T

MAKE YOUR GARDEN FEED YOU

E. T. BROWN

A concise, practical book on gardening,
poultry, rabbit-breeding, and bee-keeping
in war-time conditions.
Clearly illustrated in black and white.

Harper
Press

Harper*Press*
An imprint of HarperCollins*Publishers*
77–85 Fulham Palace Road

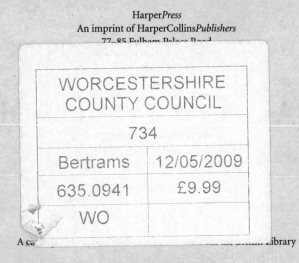
A ca.. Library

ISBN 978-0-00-731378-5

Printed and bound in Great Britain by Clays Ltd, St Ives plc

Mixed Sources
Product group from well-managed
forests and other controlled sources
www.fsc.org   Cert no. SW-COC-1806
© 1996 Forest Stewardship Council

FSC

FSC is a non-profit international organisation established to promote the
responsible management of the world's forests. Products carrying the FSC
label are independently certified to assure consumers that they come
from forests that are managed to meet the social, economic and
ecological needs of present or future generations.

Find out more about HarperCollins and the environment at
www.harpercollins.co.uk/green

HOW TO USE THIS BOOK

MANY are the difficulties that beset the person equipped for the first time with a spade, a packet of seeds, and a plot of soil. "How deep must I plant them?" "Do they need watering?" "What will they look like when they come up?" These are only a few of the questions that dismay the novice.

The experienced gardener in war-time is in little better position. He knows the way he has always gone about his tasks, he knows when to put his seeds in and what to do with the seedlings when they appear. But now he ought to ask himself: "Is my garden yielding as much per square foot as it should do?" "Am I getting the best possible results in the shortest time or could I perhaps do better if I changed my methods?" In addition, he has two very big problems—what to use for manures now that many kinds are unobtainable, and how to curtail waste which was previously unimportant but now is criminal.

Answers to all these questions could be discovered eventually by experiment—the process of trial and error. But at a time of national emergency there is neither leisure nor material for this method. The necessary information has to be acquired quickly and with the minimum of effort. *Make Your Garden Feed You* has been written to meet this need.

The book is severely practical. The author takes a plot of ground—90 feet by 60 feet—and shows exactly how it must be arranged and treated to make it yield the maximum amount of food for the minimum expenditure of money and labour. He explains why it is economical to keep fowls, rabbits, and bees, in addition to growing vegetables and fruit, and he gives sound advice on how to overcome the war-time difficulties of manuring the ground and feeding the livestock.

READ THE OPENING SECTIONS WITH CARE

The best way to use this book is to read it straight through as far as the end of the section on vegetable growing, and to spend half an hour or so absorbing the details of the plan shown on pages 2 and 3. The next step is to adapt the author's arrangement to suit your own garden or allotment. You may have to leave out the fruit trees or decide bee-keeping is unsuitable in your neighbourhood. But the main features of the scheme—especially the inclusion of three vegetable plots—can be kept for any garden, whatever its size or special peculiarities. If you only have room for one or two rows of vegetables you can plan to grow different crops from one year to the next.

CHOOSE WHAT YOU WANT FROM THE CONTENTS LIST

When you have fixed the layout for your own garden and have the preliminary details worked out, then look at the contents list on page v. This shows the range of subjects covered by the book and all you need to do is to turn to the page where your special problems are solved. How deep to dig the ground, how much seed to buy, when to put it in, when and how to transplant the seedlings—the answers to all such questions can be found immediately. Some difficulties, however, are not easy to clear up in words ; the distinction, for example, between a useful plant and a dangerous weed requires an object lesson rather than an explanation. These obstacles, therefore, are removed by a number of very clear illustrations which will be of use and interest to beginner and veteran alike.

CONTENTS

FRUIT TREES AND TOMATOES

FLOWERS TO GROW IN WAR-TIME

YOUR GARDEN FRIENDS AND FOES

YOUR JOB MONTH BY MONTH

POULTRY-KEEPING IN WAR-TIME

RABBITS FOR FLESH AND FUR

ILLUSTRATIONS

TO PLAN YOUR CROPS

WHATEVER the shape and size of your allotment or garden, you are advised to decide where everything you intend to grow is to be planted before you start. Similarly the sites of the shed, greenhouse, manure heap, etc., should all be chosen at the outset.

The diagram given here (Fig. 1) shows the layout recommended for a plot measuring 90 ft. by 60 ft. If your allotment or garden plot is smaller you should not have much difficulty in adapting the layout to suit your individual need. For instance, if your plot measures 90 ft. by 45 ft. and you propose to go in for all the four departments of food production, all it means is that the three vegetable plots will be 27 ft. by 28 ft. instead of 42 ft. by 28 ft.

IF THERE IS NO FENCE

It is to be hoped that the 90-ft. long north boundary consists of a solid fence, since this simplifies things considerably ; but if it happens to be a wire-strand fence, or even no fence at all, this little difficulty can be overcome easily enough and without the outlay of a lot of money.

Should there be no fencing, run three strands of stout wire from the greenhouse and a post in one corner to the corner of the general-purpose shed, and again from the east corner of the shed to the corner of the poultry house, covering this with 1-in. mesh, 4-ft. high wire-netting. Support by means of 3-in. square stakes placed about 5 ft. apart.

PLACING THE FRUIT TREES AND TOMATOES

Leaf-mould is invaluable, particularly in these days when stable manure is so difficult to obtain, so provision has to be made for its storage. And the same is true of the compost heap. These 6 ft. by 5 ft. areas can be fronted by 5-ft. high trellis with a bed in front for planting soft fruit climbers.

At the back of the seed-bed and between the frames and the north boundary cordon, fruit trees or tomatoes may be grown if the wall is solid. If the fence is only of wire strands, tomatoes are ruled out, because they would not be sufficiently sheltered.

It is suggested that espalier fruit trees should be planted at the north end of plots 1 and 2, and that a herb bed, 4 ft. in width, should be sown or planted at the far end of plot 3,

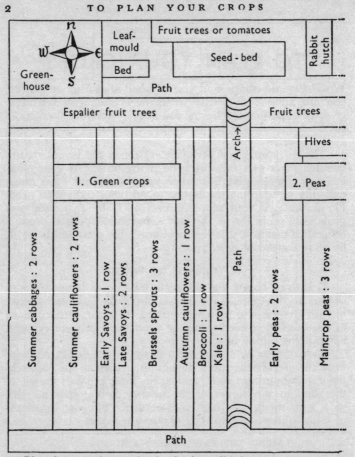

1. *Plan for a garden 90 feet by 60 feet, allowing space for chickens, rabbits, and bees. The plan can be adapted to suit individual needs, but three vegetable plots are essential for the best results.*

while to accommodate a greater number of soft fruit bushes 8 ft. or 10 ft. long pergolas—a string of connected arches—should be erected at each end of the two main paths. The bee-hives can be placed conveniently close to the fruit trees of the centre plot, where the bees will help to fertilize them.

WHY THREE VEGETABLE PLOTS ARE ESSENTIAL

Whatever else you may not do, you should divide the area to be used for growing vegetables into three separate plots. It does not matter whether these are separated by a path, as

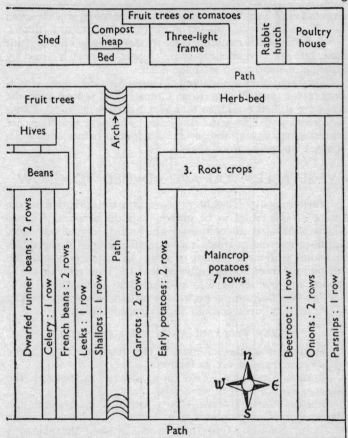

1. If flowers are grown, they should edge the vegetable plots. The arches at the ends of the centre paths can support roses or soft, climbing fruits, such as raspberries. Each path should be about 3 feet wide.

shown in the diagram, or not, but you should mark their confines in one way or another.

Much of the success that will attend your efforts depends upon planning your crops in three groups. Here are the reasons :

1. No crop should be taken off the same plot two years in succession.

2. Some crops are shallow-rooting and only take plant food from the surface, while others are deep-rooting and obtain their food from the lower soil. By arranging for a deep-rooting

crop to follow a shallow-rooting one, and *vice versa*, you are saved
spending a lot of extra money on manure or chemical fertilisers.

3. Some plants require a large quantity of one kind of plant
food, but others need little of it. Again, manure is saved by
growing one such crop after the other.

The three plots are marked : Plot 1, Green Crops; Plot 2,
Peas, etc. ; and Plot 3, Root Crops. The second year the
crops are shifted round, so that Plot 1 carries the roots, Plot 2
the greens and Plot 3 the peas, etc. The next year they are
moved a step again, and so on. Each crop comes back to its
original site every third year.

VEGETABLES YOU ARE ADVISED TO GROW

Various points have been taken into consideration in the
choice of vegetables to be grown, and the amount of space
which is devoted to each—easy cultivation, high food value,
health-promoting qualities, and a regular supply of vegetables
in season without a surplus of any. In connection with the
last point it must be remembered that the requirements of the
rabbits and poultry have to be taken into account.

The vegetables to be grown are set out below in the order
in which they are placed in their respective plots.[1]

GREEN VEGETABLES ON THE FIRST PLOT

Reading from the left side of the diagram (Fig. 1), the
crops recommended are as follows :

SUMMER CABBAGES.—Two rows, with 18 in. between the
plants, giving a total of 56 heads.

SUMMER CAULIFLOWERS.—Two rows, 18 in. between the
plants, a total of 56 plants.

EARLY SAVOYS.—One row, 15 in. between the plants, a
total of 34.

LATE SAVOYS.—Two rows, 18 in. between the plants, a
total of 56.

BRUSSELS SPROUTS.—Three rows, 2 ft. between the plants,
a total of 63.

AUTUMN CAULIFLOWERS.—One row, 2 ft. between the
plants, a total of 28.

BROCCOLI.—One row, 2 ft. between the plants, a total
of 28.

KALE OR BORECOLE.—One row, 2 ft. between the plants,
a total of 28.

These crops take a long time to grow to maturity. To
conserve valuable space, turnips, early carrots, lettuces,

[1] For quantities of seed and planting details, see pages 19, 27, 28-53.

summer spinach and salad onions should be sown between the main vegetable crops as catch-crops. These crops will all be ready for harvesting before the main vegetables attain any great size and require the space they occupied.

VEGETABLES FOR THE SECOND PLOT

On Plot 2 the crops are as follows : Early peas, 2 rows ; main-crop peas, 3 rows ; dwarfed runner beans, 2 rows ; celery (grown in a trench), 1 row ; dwarf French beans, 2 rows ; leeks, 1 row ; and shallots, 1 row. It is not possible to say how many bushels of peas and beans will be produced, but with 1 ft. between the plants there should be 42 heads of celery and, with 6 in. between the plants, there will be about 84 leeks.

Lettuces and other salad plants should be grown as a catch-crop on the ridges at each side of the celery trench, sowings being made every three weeks to provide a succession.

THE ROOT CROPS ON THE THIRD PLOT

The two rows of carrots are placed close to the path, the reason being that this crop is not thinned in the usual way, but young roots are pulled as they are required in the house. Ultimately the carrots should stand 3 in. apart, so 168 are available for storing for winter use.

Two rows of early potatoes—the new potatoes which are so acceptable after months of stored ones—should suffice for the average household. Seven rows of main-crop potatoes are allowed for, however, not only because they are wanted for many months, but so that there will be a goodly number for the fowls and, possibly, the other live stock. The 126 beetroots from the single row should prove sufficient both for pickling and cooking as a vegetable ; the 252 onions from the two rows should see the family through the winter ; and the 56 parsnips, grown 9 in. apart in the one row, is about the correct proportion for these vegetables.

These crops—with the exception of the parsnips, which are best left in the ground, at any rate until after there have been a good few frosts—are cleared off the ground some time before October, when a number of crops should be planted. When the potatoes have been gathered, two rows of broad beans should be sown and the remainder of the ground planted with spring cabbages. When the carrots, beetroots, and onions have been harvested, their places should be taken by prickly spinach and winter lettuce.

FRUITS OF THE THREE-YEAR CROPPING PLAN

If you follow the three-year cropping plan suggested above, you will never be without delicious vegetables from year end to year end. How does this succession appeal to you—and to the members of your household ?

SPRING (February 15th to May 15th).—Beetroots, broccoli, cabbages, carrots, kale, leeks, onions, parsnips, late savoys, and spinach.

SUMMER (May 15th to August 15th).—Broad, French, and runner beans, beetroots, cabbages, carrots, cauliflowers, lettuce, onions and peas.

AUTUMN (August 15th to November 15th).—Runner beans, beetroots, broccoli, brussels sprouts, carrots, cauliflowers, celery, lettuce, onions, spinach and turnips.

WINTER (November 15th to February 15th).—Beetroots, broccoli, brussels sprouts, carrots, celery, kale, leeks, onions, parsnips, early savoys, spinach and turnips.

TOOLS TO MAKE OR BUY

IF the allotment or garden plot is to be cultivated properly a certain number of tools is necessary. The list is a fairly long one, and if all are purchased by each individual gardener it runs away with a lot of money. There are certain tools which are in frequent use, such as a spade, fork and hoe, and these should certainly be bought. It is suggested, however, that many of the others might well be bought by a number of allotment-holders and used on a communal basis. Failing this, an agreement might be come to for one to purchase one or two articles, another one or two different ones, and so on. For example, a syringe, garden hose, and a spraying machine are required now and again, but not sufficiently often to warrant individual purchase.

It must be for war-time gardeners to decide which tools should be bought outright and which obtained collectively ; so perhaps it is better to enumerate the different ones and give brief particulars regarding them.

TOOLS YOU CANNOT DO WITHOUT

DIGGING TOOLS.—One of the most important duties in connection with gardening is digging, so the first requirement is a first-class spade. It is worth while spending an extra shilling or so and getting a good one. It should be of the correct weight, a point which can be ascertained after handling a few at the shop.

Two forks are really necessary. One should be a four-pronged model, with round prongs, for all ordinary purposes. The second should have flat prongs, this being wanted for lifting manure, gathering up vegetable refuse, such as potato haulm and cabbage stalks, and also for lifting potatoes. And a trowel is essential for making holes for the reception of plants raised in the seed-bed.

RAKES AND HOES.—After digging comes the preparation of the surface soil—the production of a fine tilth. A couple of iron rakes and a wooden rake (the latter for the final raking) are needed. One iron rake should be 8 in. and the other 12 in. If you can get hold of an old 12-in. iron rake accept it as a gift, break off all the teeth with the exception of the two outside ones, and you will have an excellent tool for drawing two drills at once.

Hoeing is a job which must not be neglected, so both a Dutch and a V-shaped hoe should be bought.

THE GARDEN LINE.—Some kind of a garden line is required when drawing drills. Blind cord can be used for the purpose, attached to a wooden stake at each end. But unless treated carefully the cord is liable to perish rapidly. It really pays to invest in a proper line with an iron stake at one end and a staked winder at the other. Such a line lasts for years ; the cord dries well, since the centre of the roll is hollow. Although not essential, as a 5-ft. tape measure does well enough, a 12-ft. rod marked off into feet, with the first 3 ft. marked off in inches, is useful for spacing out rows and plants.

OTHER USEFUL TOOLS

There are many occasions when a wheelbarrow is needed. One can be made at home, mounted on one or two wheels from an old perambulator ; but as they do not cost a lot the war-time gardener may decide to buy one.

Watering is another necessary duty, so the purchase of a watering-can suggests itself. A syringe is also an asset.

The tools which are only wanted occasionally, or perhaps never at all, are a hose-pipe and roller, a spraying machine, mower (not likely, as grass is at a discount in war-time), a light garden roller, secateurs, pruning-knife, hedge shears, edging shears and a garden basket.

SEED BOXES, TRAYS, PEA STICKS, AND STRING

For raising seedlings in the frame or greenhouse seed-boxes or pans are required. The former are the better. The boxes should be 15 in. long, 10 in. wide and 3 in., 4 in., and 5 in. deep. All pans and boxes must be fitted with drainage holes in the bottom.

If the amateur food-grower has a greenhouse, flower-pots must be bought. Flower-pots range from 2 in. in diameter to 18 in., but these outside measurements can be forgotten. A few sixties, forty-eights, thirty-twos, twenty-fours and sixteens should prove sufficient.

It is recommended that seed potatoes should be sprouted before being planted. Trays are used and one or two should be knocked up out of $\frac{3}{4}$-in. thick battens, 3 in. wide. The trays should be made with a sparred bottom and the two ends should be rather higher than the sides so that, when they are piled on top of each other, the contents of all receive plenty of air. These trays are also excellent for storing other things, such as onions.

Lastly, bean and pea sticks are required, but the former may be dispensed with if the runner beans are dwarfed. A ball

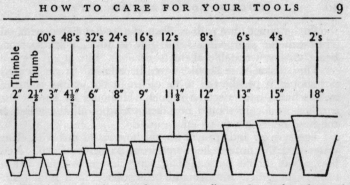

2. *Flower-pots are given numbers corresponding to the number of pots of different sizes that can be made from a cast of clay. They range in diameter from 2 inches to 18 inches ; but 3 inches to 9 inches are the sizes most often needed in the small garden.*

of fairly stout string and some raffia complete the list of things you will need to carry out all the necessary work.

HOW TO CARE FOR YOUR GARDENING TOOLS

Gardening tools cost a considerable amount of money, so it is folly to neglect them. They can all be made to give excellent service for many years if properly looked after. A golden rule to adopt is that each one should be thoroughly cleaned immediately after use and then returned to its allotted position in the general-purpose shed—a shed which should be damp-proof, if possible, and in which a tin of oil (not paraffin) and a bundle of clean rags are kept handy.

The tools which are most likely to be bought at first are those used in working the soil. A good rubbing with a piece of old sacking is usually sufficient but, if the ground happens to be very wet, the tools should be scrubbed and, after drying, they should be lightly oiled. This applies to the spade, forks, rakes, hoes, trowel, and the like. Occasionally it may be necessary to file the spade a little, because, if the ground is stony, it becomes blunt in course of time.

The garden basket—this is usually oblong in shape, rounded at the bottom and fitted with a handle for convenient carrying—is apt to get wet and dirty. It should be dried carefully if only wet, but scrubbed and dried if very muddy.

If the wheelbarrow can be kept under cover all the better, but, failing this, it should be turned upside down and a sack thrown over it. The only attention it requires is for the wheel to be oiled at frequent intervals.

The edged tools are the most expensive, so after use they

should be wiped dry with a clean rag and smeared with oil. They call for sharpening from time to time, a scythe stone being the most suitable agent to use.

The garden hose should never be allowed to get twisted, nor should it be allowed to lie about in hot, sunny weather, as this has a bad effect on rubber. It should be attached to a roller, and care should be taken to expel all the water as the hose is being wound up.

The syringe and sprayer should be washed out with clean water and the nozzles kept free from particles of grit. New flower-pots should be soaked in water for some hours before using, while dirty ones should be scrubbed in a mild disinfectant solution and rinsed in fresh water.

FRAMES AND THE GARDEN SHED

IN normal times most amateur gardeners endeavour to raise out-of-season crops, relying upon purchase for the ordinary vegetables when obtainable in the shops. The aim of the wartime gardener, however, is to produce as much food as possible, so extra early and late crops which occupy a considerable amount of room and involve a lot of work, together with the possession of a heated greenhouse or frames, need not be considered. At the same time, if the allotment already boasts a small greenhouse this should certainly be used. In any case one or two frames should be made or bought, since they are practically indispensable.

HOW TO CONSTRUCT A GARDEN FRAME

A frame is simply a box made rather higher at the back than at the front and fitted with a glass top. If the allotment or garden plot is of only small dimensions there is no reason why a crate should not be re-modelled and a piece of glass, say, a picture-frame, used for the top. Two or three such frames might be rigged up at little or no cost.

For the larger allotment, however, it is better to buy a three-light frame or, if the amateur gardener is handy with tools, to buy the "lights" and fashion the woodwork at home.

The usual type of frame is that known as the lean-to, as shown in Fig. 3. The ordinary light measures 6 ft. by 4 ft., so the whole structure measures 12 ft. by 6 ft. The body of the frame should be 14 in. high in front and 18 in. high at the back, and it should be made of sound boarding 1¼ in. in thickness. When more than one "light" is used there must be a channelled cross-member where they come together, so that

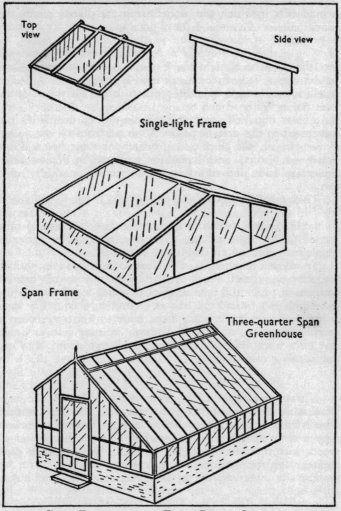

Top
view

Side view

Single-light Frame

Span Frame

Three-quarter Span
Greenhouse

3. COLD FRAMES AND A FROST-PROOF GREENHOUSE.

the rain which percolates between may drain away without
reaching the inside of the frame, where it may do damage to
young seedlings.

The series of frames should be placed directly on the
ground (slightly raised, if possible, to ensure adequate drainage)
and, if plants are to be grown in pots, pans, or seed-boxes,
filled with a 10-in. layer of cinders or coconut fibre. If a bed

is made up, in which the plants are to be placed direct, this
should consist of a 10-in. layer of good garden soil.

FOR AND AGAINST A HEATED FRAME

It is questionable whether it would pay the amateur home
food-producer to go in for one or more heated frames. A heated
frame is mostly used for raising plants in the early part of the
year before the seed can be sown outdoors so that very early
crops are obtained, and this branch of gardening is not
advocated at the present time. A heated frame is one raised
or rested on a 4-ft. thick pile of mixed horse manure and oak
and beech leaves. Stable manure is practically unprocurable
nowadays, so the use of a heated frame is automatically ruled
out.

There is, however, a suggestion which might commend
itself to the gardener who is able to obtain a small quantity
of stable manure. This is to make a sunk pit instead of a
heated frame. In most cases, however, it would be better to
employ the manure for digging into the soil.

To make a sunk pit, dig a hole 2½ ft. deep and 2 in. shorter
and narrower than the area covered by the number of " lights "
to be used. Line this with any rough, thick wood obtainable,
extending the front 4 in. above ground level and the back
8 in., with the ends sloping from back to front. Prepare a
mixture of stable manure and leaves, turning it over every
day for a week, then put this into the pit to a depth of 18 in.,
compressing each layer as it is thrown in. Cover this with
3 in. of soil and then 5 in. of ashes, cinders or coconut fibre
if seed-boxes are to be accommodated, or with 4 in. of soil
if seeds are to be sown or seedlings planted.

Frames must be ventilated as weather conditions permit.
This is done by raising the " lights " at one side—the side away
from any wind that may be blowing. To do this, blocks of
wood, cut in 1-in. steps, are needed. In unusually cold
weather the temperature in a frame may be kept warm by
putting a hot-water bottle, preferably metal, under it all night.

THREE TYPES OF FROST-PROOF GREENHOUSE

A heated greenhouse, that is, one in which a winter night
temperature of round about 50 degrees F. can be maintained,
is out of place on the war-time allotment, but a frost-proof
one can be pressed into service and put to a good use for
certain vegetable crops and for raising flowering plants for the
decoration of the house.

There are three principal types of greenhouses—the span
or gable, the three-quarter span, and the lean-to. The lean-to

(higher at the back than at the front) is excellent when the north boundary consists of a wall, say, 8 ft. or 9 ft. high. The three-quarter span (Fig. 3) is recommended when the north wall is 6 ft. to 7 ft. high. Both of these types cost less than the span house, since one side can be dispensed with altogether, but the span greenhouse is the most practical. A useful size is 10 ft. or 12 ft. in length and 8 ft. to 10 ft. in width.

A greenhouse is allowed for in the layout (Fig. 1). If one is not erected the heap of leaf-mould with trellis-backed bed in front may be moved to the west boundary and the seed-bed and row of fruit trees or tomatoes extended to cover the extra space. In this case part of the seed-bed may be used for raising a few early vegetables or flowers for cutting.

TO BUILD AND EQUIP THE GENERAL-PURPOSE SHED

A tool-shed for storing the implements so that they are not left out in the open is a necessity on the allotment. If poultry, rabbits and bees are also kept as recommended, the tool-shed should be large enough to be used as a general-purpose shed. A convenient size is 16 ft. long by 8 ft. wide.

This shed need not be an expensive structure and, although made of surplus material, neither need it be unsightly. It should be lean-to in form, say, 6 ft. high at the back and 8 ft. high in front. There should be a door in the front—the centre is the best position—and large windows on each side.

Such a shed can be built of plywood obtained from tea-chests, timber from crates and boxes, composite board, or even a high-grade bitumen felt, on a framework of wood. Corrugated iron is a durable, not-too-expensive, roofing material. The corner uprights should be of 3 in. by 3 in. battens (natural poles of 2½-in. or 3-in. diameter may be used if obtainable) and the intermediate uprights and the horizontals of 2 in. by 2 in. material, with 3 in. by 1 in. battens placed on edge for the rafters.

The exact positioning of the shed fitments is left to the individual, but one or two points may be briefly discussed.

1. Under each window there should be a table about 2 ft. in width, with a series of drawers below.

2. There should be plenty of hooks and nails on the walls, so that gardening tools and other articles may be hung up, with shelves above for storing some of the smaller utensils.

3. If any poultry food is stored in this shed, suitable bins can be made out of tea-chests, barrels or crates, but the most satisfactory container is the galvanised iron dustbin. If the shed floor is of natural earth the food receptacles should be stood on a slatted platform to preserve them from damp.

SPADE-WORK AND SOWING

In many districts the local authorities are taking over large tracts of land and converting them into allotments. As a general rule, the area is simply measured off into plots, and those who take them over have to do all the necessary " spade-work " ; and spade-work it is, in very truth. Before dealing with the usual routine work connected with vegetable-growing it may be advisable to say something regarding the best way of turning a piece of rough land into an allotment.

Quite apart from the nature and texture of the land itself its condition must be considered. The new allotment site may be either a piece of old grassland or waste ground. These require rather different treatment to bring them into a productive state.

If the area of ground allotted to you consists of turfed land, the first job is to remove the sods. This means a considerable amount of work, but one is repaid handsomely, since the turves as they are removed can be heaped up in a corner of the plot and converted into an excellent manure substitute in about six months' time. The turves and the soil below are almost certain, however, to be infested with wire-worms and similar pests, so thorough fumigation of the former as they are stacked up and of the latter when it is being dug is essential.[1]

HOW TO DISCOVER THE QUALITY OF THE SOIL

The next thing to do is to find out the nature of the soil, because the preparation of the allotment depends largely upon this. Two or three holes should be dug in different parts and the sides examined. It is quite easy to see how deep is the layer of top soil (this should be good) and what lies below, whether fairly good soil, gravel or clay.

The holder of a new allotment will find it best to put in a lot of work digging the whole plot at the start, so it is advised that full trenching should be adopted. There are two methods of full trenching[2]—working the soil to a depth of about 3 ft.—and which one should be followed must be decided when the nature of the soil is known.

If the top soil (this may be of any depth from a few inches to a foot) is vastly better than the subsoil (the second spit or foot) the ground should be trenched so that the top soil is kept on top and the subsoil beneath. If, however, the good

[1] See page 77.   [2] See page 18.

soil goes down to a depth of 2 ft., the second method is better, in which case the top soil becomes the subsoil and the subsoil the top soil. Weather action thus benefits the former subsoil.

TO CLEAN THE LAND

As digging proceeds all stones should be collected and all deep-rooting perennial weeds like dandelions and plantains should be removed since, even if only bits of root are left in the ground, they will spring up again. These perennial weeds should be burned out-of-hand and not allowed to rot down.

If the site has previously been waste land the surface is sure to be covered with stones and other forms of rubbish— some of it too finely powdered to allow it to be removed. After gathering up the larger material the area should be full-trenched by the second method, so that the remaining rubbish is buried a foot below the surface.

WHY PATHS ARE NECESSARY

If the allotment measures, say, 90 ft. by 60 ft., it is really necessary to have a number of paths, and the better these are constructed the easier the work of the gardener, since work has often to be done in bad weather. In any case, no matter what the paths consist of, it is advisable to have a definite edging. The vegetable plots are naturally raised a little above the level of the paths owing to the cultivation of the ground so, unless a proper edging is provided, the soil gets on to the paths, making the allotment look untidy and uncared-for.

Various materials can be used for separating the plots from the paths, such as tiles, bricks, concrete slabs or wood. The last mentioned is excellent and is possibly the least expensive. The timber should be 5 in. wide and 1 in. thick, and 400 ft. is required for a plot 90 ft. by 60 ft. It may just happen, however, that in some districts one of the other three materials can be obtained even more cheaply, in which case it should be used.

In addition to the permanent edging there is no reason why a " live " edging should not be planted. The dwarf plants used for the purpose occupy very little space and yet they make the allotment more attractive and also provide a few cut flowers for home decoration. Among the plants which are recommended for this purpose are : Gold Dust (*Alyssum saxatile compactum*), Alkanet (*Anchusa myosotidiflora*), Rock Cress (*Arabis albida*), Thrift (*Armeria maritima*), Bellflower (*Campanula*) and Evergreen Candytuft (*Iberis sempervirens*).

MAKING THE PATHS

Naturally enough the allotment-holder does not wish to spend a penny more than necessary, so it is not advised that the best of all path-making materials—gravel—should be used. On no account, however, should the natural grass be retained on the paths, since it requires a lot of attention, while it is also too good a harbourage for snails and slugs.

The grass should be skimmed off, and if cinders, clinkers, chippings, and ashes (coal ashes damped with tar make a particularly durable path) cannot be obtained, the ground should just be rounded off a little, so that it is slightly higher in the centre, and then rolled. It is worth while for the amateur gardener to make a few inquiries locally, because it is often possible to secure a sufficient quantity of clinkers or similar material for next to nothing, save the cost of carting. A 3-in. layer of any available material is ample.

GOLDEN RULES FOR DIGGING

Most amateur gardeners make digging a very laborious task. It certainly calls for the expenditure of a certain amount of elbow grease, but it is not really hard work—when done in the proper way.

There are three methods of digging—single-spit, double digging and trenching, these working the soil to a depth of 1 ft., 2 ft. and 3 ft. respectively. There are golden rules which can be applied to all.

1. Have a spade of the right weight and keep it sharp and clean.

2. Drive the spade vertically into the ground, using the foot to give added pressure as necessary.

3. Always work with a trench in front, for this not only makes it easier to incorporate manure and decayed vegetable refuse with the soil, since they can be thoroughly mixed in the trench, but also makes the actual digging lighter work.

SINGLE-SPIT DIGGING

In single-spit digging excavate a trench 1 ft. deep (the exact depth should depend upon whether the soil is uniformly good down to this maximum depth) and 1 ft. wide, and remove the soil to the other end of the plot. Six inches away from the edge of the trench insert the spade, lift up a spadeful of mould and throw it into the far side of the trench, breaking up the lumps at the same time. Use the excavated soil for

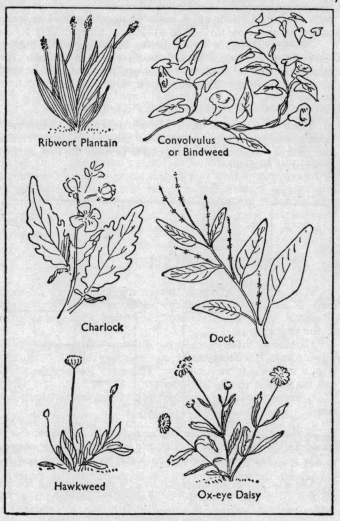

Ribwort Plantain

Convolvulus
or Bindweed

Charlock

Dock

Hawkweed

Ox-eye Daisy

4. WEEDS THAT MUST BE DUG UP AND BURNT.

filling the trench which remains when digging is completed.

DOUBLE DIGGING OR MOCK-TRENCHING

Double digging is practically the same as single-spit digging but, when the trench is opened, the subsoil or second spit of soil should be thoroughly broken up with the fork, and as each section of under-soil is revealed it, too, should be forked over. In this way the soil is worked to a depth of 2 ft.

Double digging is much better than single-spit digging, since the soil is better aerated, water can pass through more easily, and the roots of the plants can penetrate more deeply in search of food. This method is shown in Fig. 5.

THE TWO METHODS OF FULL TRENCHING

There are two methods of full trenching. The first is usually employed, and always when the top soil is better than the subsoil. To trench the vegetable plot by the first method, proceed as follows :

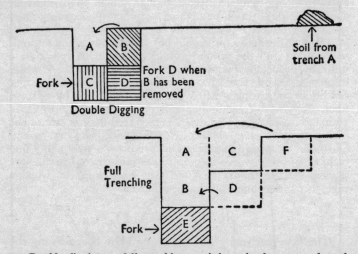

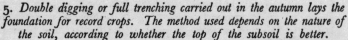

5. *Double digging or full trenching carried out in the autumn lays the foundation for record crops. The method used depends on the nature of the soil, according to whether the top of the subsoil is better.*

Dig out a 2-ft. wide trench of top soil, removing the soil to the other end of the plot. Follow by taking out a 1-ft. wide trench of subsoil, as shown at B in Fig. 2, removing to the other end, but keeping it separate. Then fork over the third spit of soil (E). Continue by digging one-half of D and throwing it into the back of B ; follow with the other half of D, so that B is filled. Next throw one-half of F on top of B at A, then the other half. The subsoil exposed by the removal of D should then be forked over. At the end of the plot the two heaps of excavated soil are used for filling the trench.

In the second method, after taking out a 2-ft. wide trench

of top soil, follow with a 2-ft. wide trench of subsoil and fork
up the third spit. Then throw the next 2 ft. of top soil into
the bottom of the trench and cover this with the 2 ft. of subsoil, and again fork over the exposed third spit of soil. At the
end of the plot put the excavated top soil in the bottom of
the trench and cover with the excavated subsoil.

THE ART OF FRUITFUL SOWING

Practically all of the crops grown in the war-time gardener's
allotment or garden plot are raised from seeds sown in the
open. Sowing, while a simple enough job in itself, must be
done in the right way if bumper crops of first-quality vegetables
are to be produced. It will repay careful study to learn the art.

Digging is usually (or should be) carried out in the autumn
and winter, and the ground should be left in its rough state
until shortly before it is to be sown or planted. As the weather
improves, the soil should be worked into more or less the proper
condition for sowing. After the frosts and snow have acted
upon the clods of earth they can be broken up quite easily
with the iron rake. The site, whether seed-bed or one of the
main vegetable plots, should be raked twice from end to end
and twice from side to side. This produces a reasonably fine
tilth, or in other words the top soil is pulverised. Just before
sowing the site should be gone over once with the wooden
rake, any little stones thus being removed.

TO SOW IN DRILLS

The lazy gardener's way of sowing is by broadcasting the
seed, but it is much better, although involving a little more
work, to sow in properly drawn drills. Definite rows look
better, the hoe can be worked more easily between the plants,
thinning is facilitated and the seedlings can be protected, if
necessary, by pushing up the soil on each side of the rows
to a height of, say, 3 in.

Drill sowing should be adopted, but the drills must be
drawn properly. This is the way to cut them. Stretch the
garden line along the row in which the seeds are to be sown.
Walking backwards, with one foot on the line to prevent it
moving, make a V-shaped channel the necessary depth with
the corner of the rake, a corner of the draw-hoe, or the home-
made two-teethed rake to make two drills at once. Great
care is necessary to cut the drills exactly the same depth
throughout, otherwise an uneven row of seedlings will result.

THE PROFESSIONAL SOWS THIS WAY

You will buy your small seeds in little packets or envelopes. Taking the line of least resistance, you will probably feel tempted to tear off a corner of the packet and try to trickle the seeds out in a continuous even line along the bottom of the drill. It sounds easy, but in fact your trickle will be anything but even and continuous, for the seeds will come out in little bunches. And what a lot of extra thinning you will have to do later on !

The professional goes to work in quite a different way. If the ground is dry he pours water along each drill a few hours beforehand. Then when everything is set he takes a little of the seed into the palm of his hand, stoops down and, with knuckles facing downwards and the point of the thumb directed towards the centre of the drill, proceeds to roll out a seed at a time at any distance he desires. He saves seeds and reduces thinning to the absolute minimum.

HOW TO SOW SEEDS IN BOXES

If seedlings are to be raised under glass the seed should be sown in boxes, pans, or flower-pots. The drainage holes should be covered first with a few bits of broken pot and then with a little coarse soil. The boxes or pots should then be filled with the compost or soil advised for the crop in question. The surface of the soil should be watered lightly a couple of hours beforehand, the seed sprinkled thinly on the surface and covered with a thin layer of soil.

The soil should be kept uniformly moist and the boxes kept close to the glass. The seedlings must be hardened off by keeping them under more and more natural conditions before being planted out in the open.

PLANTING, HOEING, WATERING

Cabbages and other members of the same family are sown in the seed-bed and transferred to their permanent quarters when the site apportioned to them becomes vacant and the weather conditions permit. Seedlings raised under glass must also be planted out in the open.

Planting is a very simple operation. The drills in which the seed has been sown, or the soil in the seed-boxes, should be well watered the day before so that the young plants can be lifted without damaging their roots. Holes should be opened with the trowel and, if the soil is dry, each one filled with water a few hours before a plant is inserted in each. After planting, the soil should be made firm round the stems, and the row watered. By the way, to lift seedlings out of boxes it is better to break off one side. This can be nailed on again afterwards, so the box is not ruined.

THE NEED FOR FREQUENT HOEING

Whenever the war-time gardener has a little time to spare he should wield the hoe. Hoeing is a very important cultivation operation and the more often it is conducted the better. Hoeing reduces the surface soil to a fine tilth—that is the whole object. Unless the surface soil is worked frequently, minute channels form from the under-soil to the surface and this allows the moisture in the soil to evaporate. Hoeing closes these minute tubes and so conserves moisture.

Hoeing is light work and it saves having to engage in more strenuous labour. Without hoeing the watering-can or the hose-pipe must be used much more often, and this usually means carrying the water a considerable distance on the allotment, since main water is not usually laid on.

A further advantage of applying the hoe is that it kills off small annual weeds, that is, weeds which seed themselves and so come up year after year. Weeds require food as well as the crops you grow, so eradicating them means a greater store of plant food which can be converted into an edible crop. And as you will gather later, the supplying of plant food, or manuring, is no easy task nowadays.

WHEN TO WATER AND HOW TO DO IT

However assiduously the gardener hoes his vegetable plots, a certain amount of watering is essential in dry weather. It should be remembered, however, that, while the soil may appear to be bone dry on the surface, it may be fairly moist a couple of inches or so below. Turn up a little soil or push in a finger to determine whether additional water is required.

The only thing that need be said regarding the application of water is that sprinkling the ground is worse than useless ; give it a good soaking, for this alone benefits the crops. A sprinkling tends to cause the roots of the plants to come upwards so that they can make use of the moisture and, being close to the surface, they may easily be burned when the sun is shining brightly. Water occasionally and water liberally is the best advice that can be given.

THE A. B. C. OF MANURING

Manuring, or the provision of plant food, is an absolute necessity in gardening. Without it good results over a period of years are impossible. Farmyard manure, or an efficient substitute, must be incorporated with the soil. These natural substances not only feed the plants but, as they decay, they increase the store of humus (decayed organic material) and humus is the very essence of fertility. It binds the soil together, but at the same time it leaves it porous so that air is freely admitted and water can percolate through it ; it warms the soil and it helps it to retain moisture. Farmyard manure (stable, cow, and pig) also contains millions and billions of bacteria, and these play a highly important part by their action of liberating plant food.

When natural manures are available they should be applied at the rate of one barrowload to every ten square yards. Stable manure is better for heavy land, and cow and pig manures for light.

While it is true that horses are being used more at the present time, owing to petrol rationing, the majority of gardeners will find it extremely difficult to obtain supplies of horse manure. The ordinary gardener is faced with a difficulty in this connection, because it means running the place with very little or no natural manure. Humus must, however, be provided, or sooner or later the soil will show definite signs of weakness and the crops will consequently suffer.

TO USE MANURE FROM POULTRY AND RABBITS

Natural manures may not be obtainable, but all vegetable matter is capable of supplying humus, so the war-time gardener must take stock of what is available in his own district. But before dealing with the numerous substitutes which can be used successfully something may be said about the two manures which are produced by poultry and rabbits.

Poultry manure is first-class. When fowls are kept on the intensive system in a scratching-shed the droppings are available in two forms. There are the neat droppings (or mixed with a little dry earth or sand) from the droppings-board placed beneath the perches ; there is also the manure-impregnated litter from the poultry-house floor. The latter is invaluable for digging into the soil in the autumn or winter when the vegetable plots are being treated to their annual digging, a useful dressing being 1 cwt. to one-sixth of an acre. The straw or dried leaves used as litter supply humus ; the droppings supply other plant foods, nitrogen, potash and phosphorus. But since poultry manure is rather deficient in the last-mentioned, it is advisable to add a fifth part by weight of mineral superphosphates to the litter manure.

The neat droppings are best used for top-dressing ; that is, applying to the crops as they are actually growing, in the same way as chemical fertilisers are employed. A satisfactory dressing is ½ oz. per yard of row.

Rabbit manure is not very rich in plant food, but it is very durable and so supplies nourishment for many months on end. It should be dug into the soil in the autumn or winter at the rate of 28 lb. per rod. It will be necessary to collect this manure for a whole year as it is only applied at digging time in the autumn or winter. To store it, cover with vegetable refuse or mix with the compost heap.

TO OBTAIN AND STORE LEAF-MOULD AND COMPOST

Every opportunity should be taken in the late summer and autumn of collecting fallen leaves. These, when properly rotted down, become what is known as leaf-mould, which is first-class for many different purposes. The leaves as they are collected should be heaped up on a site reserved for them and covered with wire-netting to prevent them being blown all over the place. They should be allowed to remain for ten to twelve months. There is just one point in connection with the making of leaf-mould. *Oak and beech leaves should not be added to the heap.* They should be reserved for making the hot-bed in the sunk pit, if one is made, or failing this they should not be gathered.

Right throughout the year there is a supply of waste or refuse vegetable stuff ; material which is not good enough for the house and not even suitable for the fowls and rabbits. Although unfit for consumption it should certainly not be thrown away, since most of it can be converted into valuable plant food and humus provider with little trouble.

When the various plots are being cleared it will be found that there are two different kinds of refuse. Some of it, like cabbage stumps, does not rot down, but much is soft and succulent and decays rapidly. The former should be consigned to the bonfire—the resulting ashes are extremely useful —but the latter should be stacked. There are two ways of doing this. A heap can be formed on the ground surface, or a hole can be dug and the soft material thrown therein. A 6 ft. by 5 ft. area provides a suitable place, and it is suggested that as there is usually a considerable quantity of refuse to deal with, a pit should be dug.

As the refuse is gathered—surface-rooting weeds, turnip and carrot-tops and the like—it should be deposited in the pit, and now and again a few shovelsful of soil should be scattered on top. In the ordinary garden it is possible to improve the compost greatly by throwing on all the household " slops," including soapy water, but this is not a practical suggestion when the allotment is some distance from the house. To obviate any unpleasant odour a little lime may be scattered over the refuse occasionally.

SUBSTITUTES FOR FARMYARD MANURE

One of the best substitutes for farmyard manure is hop manure. There are numerous proprietary manures of this description ; all have spent hops as the basis (these supply humus) together with various chemicals. They are excellent, while they are easy and clean to handle and apply. They should be used at the rate advised by the vendors.

Many different kinds of organic refuse are converted into manure. They include shoddy, leather dust, damaged cattle cakes, rape dust, cotton-seed dust, feather waste, hair waste, hoof and horn waste, and so on. The amateur gardener should make inquiries in his own district concerning whether any of these are obtainable. If so they should be applied and dug into the soil in the autumn or winter in the same way as natural manure and at the same rate—three barrowloads to the rod.

Those who live near a large town or in a city may be able to obtain regular supplies of sewage. The solid matter is extracted and usually mixed with lime, alumina, and other chemicals and disposed of to agriculturists. It is usually obtainable in two forms—sludge which is something like soft clay, or dried and ground into a fine powder. The former is the better. It should be applied at the rate of 4 cwt. to the rod and dug in during the winter, preferably after it has lain on the surface for a short time and been subjected to a few frosts.

Gardeners living at the seaside may be able to collect seaweed. This is excellent and about equal in value to farmyard manure. It should be stacked up and allowed to rot down. Apply and dig into the soil in the autumn or winter.

GREEN MANURING

Green manuring is a highly satisfactory way of increasing the fertility of the soil and increasing its humus content. It can, however, be practised to only a limited extent in the garden or on the allotment, since it implies leaving the ground

vacant for eight to ten weeks. If you are making a new allotment, however, where the ground is not particularly rich and
planting or sowing is not to be carried out for a while, green
manuring is recommended.

The surface of the area should be reduced to as fine a tilth
as possible, mustard seed broadcast thickly (this must not be
confused with the mustard of mustard and cress, for it is the
agricultural variety), and in seven or eight weeks the resulting
crop should be rolled or trodden flat and then dug well down
into the land and covered with a good layer of soil.

ARTIFICIAL MANURES AND CHEMICAL FERTILISERS

Artificial manures can be divided into two classes. Some
of them are slow-acting and this necessitates their being dug
into the soil in the autumn or winter, while others are quick-
acting and these are applied during the growing period.

Among the slow-acting chemicals basic slag, steamed bone-
meal, and bone-meal provide phosphates, and kainit and
sulphate of potash supply potash. These chemicals should be
scattered over the surface of the soil after digging is completed and then pricked in with a fork so that they are mixed
with the top two or three inches of soil.

Of the quick-acting artificials, superphosphate of lime
supplies phosphates, sulphate of ammonia and nitrate of soda
are nitrogenous foods, and guano is a good fertiliser.

The rate at which these chemicals should be applied and
the crops for which they are most suitable, together with
general mixtures which can be prepared at home, are detailed
later under the various crop headings.

SOOT DETERS INSECT PESTS

Soot is valuable as a plant food, is a grand deterrent to
insect pests, and is also a heavy-soil lightener. It contains a
fair quantity of potash, and it may be dug into the soil in the
autumn or used as a top-dressing during the spring and
summer. Fresh soot should not be used, however ; it should
first be stored for a couple of months.

TO MAKE AND USE LIQUID MANURE

Liquid manure is beneficial to a number of vegetable crops.
This does not refer to the liquid excreted by animals, but consists of a solution of the soluble ingredients of different natural
manures. Horse droppings, cow and pig manures, poultry
and rabbit manure can all be used. A bushel of the available
natural manure, or a mixture of them, is placed into a sack
and suspended in a barrel of water. In a few days the water

may be used, but it must be diluted first so that it assumes the colour of weak tea. As some of the liquid is taken out plain water should be added. After a time, when the strength of the manure water is becoming weak, the sack may be squeezed against the side of the barrel. This extracts the remainder of the soluble plant food.

Soot water can be made in the same way, but if the garden is only a fairly small one it is usually more practical to use one-half natural manure and one-half soot together.

LIME AND LIMING

Lime must be present in the soil ; it neutralises acidity or sourness, it helps to break up stiff clay and to bind very light soil. It is a plant food, but it plays a much more important part than providing nutriment. It sets free food matter from the humus and it helps bacteria in their work of converting insoluble plant food into a soluble form. It is also a soil tonic, for it makes the land a healthy place in which the plants can grow steadily, and helps to prevent disease.

As a general rule lime should be applied every third year, but never at the same time as natural manure.

Lime can be obtained in many different forms. The following are all satisfactory :

1. Chalk, broken into small pieces and dug in at the rate of 1 lb. per square yard.

2. Gas lime. This should be weathered for three or four weeks by exposure to the air, scattered on the surface at the rate of 1 lb. per square yard, and dug in.

3. Ground lime, which should be distributed over the surface after digging, using ½ lb. per square yard.

4. Limestone, which should be used as chalk.

5. Quicklime. This must be stacked in small heaps and slaked ; then it should be scattered all over the surface at the rate of ½ lb. per square yard, and dug in.

6. Slaked lime. This should be evenly distributed, using 1 lb. per square yard, and dug in.

Do not bury lime deeply. It tends to sink through the soil, so it should just be pricked into the top two or three inches.

If a three-year cropping plan[1] is adopted, one plot should be given a full dressing of natural manure or a manure substitute, the second plot a half-dressing and the third plot left unmanured each year. The lime should be applied to the unmanured plot—that is once every three years.

[1] See page 2.

THE VEGETABLE BEDS

NOTE.—*For every vegetable there are dozens of named varieties, all of them very nearly equally excellent provided they are properly handled and given the conditions they need. Moreover, every gardener with the smallest experience has his own favourites, knowing very well which varieties he considers give the best results. Particular varieties, therefore, are not, in general, given here, and any gardener desiring information on this point should take the advice of his seed merchant.*

SOME vegetables are best sown where they will come to maturity ; others should be sown in a seed-bed. The former include the root crops, peas, beans, lettuce, spinach and the like. The cabbage family—a term which comprises cabbages, cauliflowers, savoys, brussels sprouts, broccoli and kale—should always be sown in a special seed-bed and transplanted later when weather permits and space can be found for them in the plot allotted to them.

All members of the cabbage family, with the one exception of kale, are very greedy feeders. They require a large quantity of food and this you have to supply. The plot should be deeply dug and liberally manured. If you can get stable manure, work three barrowloads into every thirty square yards ; that is, twelve barrowloads into plot 1, but omitting the strip to be planted with kale. You will have to feed the plants somehow or other, so if stable manure is short use well-decayed garden refuse from the compost heap. The plants will require extra nourishment, but the chemicals to use are given under the various crop headings.

In every case the right amount of seed to sow is $\frac{1}{4}$ oz. for each 42-ft. row, so how much you have to buy depends upon the number of rows to be planted. To save you figuring this out, the necessary quantity is given for each green crop. You can make do with slightly less, so if your rows are only 25 ft. long, $\frac{1}{8}$ oz. of seed will see you through.

FROM SEED-BED TO PLOT

When the seedlings are large enough to handle safely, or when the site is vacant, they must be transferred to their permanent quarters. This planting-out is a simple enough job, but do see that you do it correctly,[1] because such a lot depends upon your adopting the correct procedure.

See page 20.

But there is a special task to be performed when transplanting members of the cabbage family. All of them are subject to two diseases—the cabbage maggot and club-root. You must examine every individual root before it is transplanted. If the root is knobbly, one of the knobs should be cut open. If the trouble is due to the presence of a maggot this will be seen—it is whitish-grey in colour. Burn all plants with such knobs and dip the roots of the remainder into a paint-like mixture of clay, water, and a little carbolic acid.

If there is no maggot it is a case of club-root. Again, burn all the plants with knobbly roots and dip the others into a mixture of soot, lime, and clay, mixed with water.

Give the plot a good dusting with lime and fork this lightly into the top 2 in. of surface soil—an excellent preventive.

CAULIFLOWERS AND CABBAGES

BROCCOLI.—This crop may be regarded as a winter edition of the cauliflower because it is in season from October onwards. As some of the summer cauliflowers may not mature so rapidly as the bulk of them, one row of broccoli with its 28 plants (2 ft. apart) is all that should be required. The same quantity of seed—$\frac{1}{4}$ oz.—is needed, this being sown in the seed-bed during the first half of April.

The soil, as for cauliflowers, should be deeply dug and well manured in the autumn or winter, and before planting out the young plants the soil should be firmed and the top 2 in. loosened. If the soil is poor apply superphosphates, $1\frac{1}{2}$ oz. and sulphate of potash, $\frac{1}{2}$ oz., to the square yard. As a genera. rule, it is not necessary to feed broccoli during the growing period, as they should be encouraged to grow on steadily without forcing so that large curds are formed by October.

In a normal winter we seldom get any severe frosts before the turn of the year, so the curds are not likely to suffer ; but should it happen that there is a very cold spell one or two leaves should be broken over. After Christmas, if there are still some good plants left and the weather is frosty, they should be lifted, roots and all, and hung upside down in the shed, where they will keep until required.

BRUSSELS SPROUTS FROM SEPTEMBER TO MARCH

BRUSSELS SPROUTS.—Brussels sprouts are so popular and their cropping season is such a long one—from September onwards, often right on into March—that it is suggested there should be three rows. As there should be 2 ft. between the plants, $\frac{1}{2}$ oz. of seed sown in the seed-bed during the first or second week of April will provide plenty of picked plants for transplanting later on.

The site should be deeply dug and well manured previously, but before planting the soil should be firmed and then the top 2 in. loosened with the fork. If the soil is on the poor side, dress as for early savoys with superphosphates and sulphate of potash, and feed in monthly instalments afterwards with sulphate of ammonia, $\frac{1}{2}$ oz. per square yard.

These plants grow to a considerable size and they must be visited frequently to pick the buttons, so there should be $2\frac{1}{4}$ ft. between the rows.

SUMMER CABBAGES.—If you live in a favoured district and the seed-bed is particularly well protected from north and east winds, you can sow cabbage seed towards the end of March, but it is usually necessary to wait for the first opportunity when soil and weather conditions permit during the first half of April. For the two rows $\frac{1}{2}$ oz. of seed will prove ample.

Cabbages, in fact all members of the same family, thrive well on any garden soil, but if yours should happen to be very heavy and rather damp you can improve it greatly by working in some leaf-mould, road grit, sand or other lightening material.

If you have an idea that the soil is not particularly good— if, for instance, the site was not manured or given a dressing of decayed vegetable refuse in the autumn or winter—or if the allotment is a new one, dress the plot with a mixture of basic slag, 3 parts by weight and kainit, $1\frac{1}{2}$ parts, using $1\frac{1}{2}$ lb. to every 10 square yards at planting time.

Plant the first row 1 ft. away from the edge of the plot, and the second row 2 ft. away from the first, putting in the plants 18 in. apart.

CABBAGES NEED LIBERAL FEEDING

Cabbages want a great deal of nitrogenous food, so once a month during the growing period make an application of not more than $\frac{1}{2}$ oz. of sulphate of ammonia to the square yard.

Given a normal season, you will be cutting your first summer cabbage at the beginning of July. Keep your eye on this crop at this time, because a few of the plants may start growing from the centre instead of forming compact heads. This is known as bolting. If only three or four adopt this irregular method of growth you can use them for the live stock ; if a large proportion, just pierce the stalk of each one close to the soil and insert a wooden match stalk.

SUMMER CAULIFLOWERS.—Unless the district is a very mild and sheltered one, in which case the seed should be sown in the seed-bed towards the end of February, it is better to buy plants from a neighbouring nurseryman. Under ordinary conditions it is necessary to sow the seed under glass—in a heated frame or greenhouse—some time in February, but in war-time the necessary equipment may not be available.

For a couple of rows you will have to buy 5 doz. plants, as they have to be planted 18 in. apart. The first row should be 2 ft. from the second row of summer cabbage and the second row another 2 ft. distance.

Just before planting it is advisable, if the land is poor, to dress the site with a mixture of equal weights of superphosphates and kainit, using 1½ lb. to every 10 square yards. During the active growing period make a monthly application of ½ oz. nitrate of soda to the square yard.

The first of the summer cauliflowers should be large enough to cut some time in June. As they cannot all be eaten at once there is a risk that too many of them reach maturity at the same time. To check this tendency break a leaf over the curd, and you will be cutting good heads for some weeks longer.

AUTUMN CAULIFLOWERS.—Although the autumn cauliflowers are in season from the beginning of September until about the end of October (into November when the autumn is a mild one) it is suggested that one row should prove sufficient, since there is a number of other vegetables available at the same time. One-quarter of an ounce of seed sown in the seed-bed towards the end of March is enough. Cultural details are the same as for summer cauliflowers.

A RELIABLE WINTER GREEN

KALE (BORECOLE).—The last green crop to be grown is Kale. There are numerous sorts, but perhaps the most useful is Scotch Curled. There should not be any scarcity of greens during the winter, but a row of kale is advised since it stands the winter better than other members of the cabbage family ; in fact, the flavour is improved when the plants are subjected to frosts.

Sowing is carried out in the seed-bed at the same time as with the majority of the members of the cabbage family, that is, in the beginning of April, while ¼ oz. of seed produces plenty of plants.

The soil does not require any special preparation, but deep digging wifhout the application of manure is recommended, particularly as kale follows a crop for which the ground was well manured. As kale grows to a considerable size, allow 2 ft. between the plants.

EARLY SAVOYS.—Following the summer cauliflowers you are going to have one row of early savoys. Sow ¼ oz. of seed in the seed-bed in the beginning of April. Savoys must be grown in soil which is deeply dug and well manured the autumn or winter before they are planted out. Before planting, however, the soil must be made firm and then the top 2 in. forked lightly over.

If the land is poor, work into the top 6 in. of soil a mixture of superphosphates, 2 oz., and sulphate of potash, ¾ oz. per square yard. During the growing period, give a dressing of ½ oz. of sulphate of ammonia per square yard once a month. Plant the row 2 ft. from the summer cauliflowers and space the plants 15 in. asunder.

These early savoys start you off on the winter well, for they are available from the beginning of November and last —unless you have eaten them all—until about the middle of January.

LATE SAVOYS.—The late savoys are wanted to carry the household on from the middle of January, when the early ones are finished, until between the end of February and the middle of March. Sowing—in the seed-bed—should be delayed until some time in May, and ½ oz. of seed will give more than enough plants for the two rows.

Treat the land in the same way as for the early savoys, and put in the plants 18 in. apart with 1 ft. between the rows. Feed during the growing period on sulphate of ammonia.

FROM PEAS TO SHALLOTS

PLOT 2 should be devoted to peas, beans, celery, leeks and shallots during the first season. It will be seen from the layout (Fig. 1) that it is planned to have 2 rows of early peas, 3 rows of main-crop peas, 2 rows of dwarfed runner beans, 1 row of celery, 2 rows of French beans, 1 row of leeks and 1 row of shallots. This division of the plot appears to be about right for the production of a succession of these vegetables for the average family. The number of rows can, of course, be altered according to circumstances, but such alteration must be left to the individual gardener.

CELERY.—It helps considerably if celery can be sown in

early February under glass and the seedlings transplanted into other boxes, 2 in. apart, as soon as they are large enough to handle, and then planted out in the prepared trench about the beginning of June, or a week or two earlier if the weather is favourable.

The majority of gardeners will, however, have to sow in the open. Sowing in a warm, sunny seed-bed in April, say, during the second week, provides excellent plants for transplanting 1 ft. apart later on in the trench.

A quarter of an ounce of seed is sufficient, whether the celery is raised under glass or in the open. The household demand for celery varies considerably, so it is for the gardener to decide whether this crop is grown in a single or double row. A double row is better than two single ones, if a fairly large crop is wanted, because it saves space.

If a single row, the trench should be 1 ft. in width ; if a double row 18 in. suffices.

PREPARING A TRENCH FOR CELERY

To make the trench, first remove the top soil and form it into a ridge on one side of the trench—the west side for preference. Fork over the second spit of soil and work in a liberal dressing of well-rotted manure or manure substitute and in addition, 1 oz. each of kainit and superphosphates to every 10 ft. of trench. Leave the trench as it is until the celery plants are ready for inserting, but flatten the top of the ridge of top soil, because it should be planted with a catch-crop.

Celery must be earthed-up as it grows. A little soil should be drawn down from the ridge—the catch-crop should be finished by this time—and worked all round the stems or stalks, but be careful not to allow any of the soil to get into the head. October is usually the month when earthing-up should begin.

FRENCH BEANS.—One row of French beans should be sown in May and the second in June. The soil should be deeply dug and heavily manured, while the addition of 1 oz. of kainit per square yard of top soil may well be applied at digging time if a manure substitute is used in place of natural manure.

The dwarf variety of French bean is recommended, ½ pint of seed being necessary for each row. The seed should be sown 3 in. apart and 2 in. deep on light soil, and 1½ in. deep on heavy soil.

Like runner beans, French beans respond to weekly doses

of liquid manure, the first being given when the first pods have set.

LEEKS.—If exceptionally large leeks are wanted, sow the seed under glass early in the year, but, failing this, a sowing in the open towards the end of February or the beginning of March produces good plants. Half an ounce of seed is all that is required for a single row. The seed should be sown $\frac{1}{4}$ in. deep in light soil or $\frac{1}{8}$ in. deep in heavy soil.

Any ordinary soil is good enough for this crop, but it is essential that it be dug deeply and that it contain plenty of humus. Again it is suggested that trench-growing is desirable, since earthing-up is advisable.

Take out a trench a spade's width and depth, put in manure or an efficient manure substitute, and then 3 in. of soil, so that, after treading, the level of the trench is 6 in. below the surrounding ground. This allows for easy earthing-up and also permits of catch-cropping, since the first earthing-up is not due until about September, with a second one during October.

After the plants have been transplanted 8 in. apart, top-dressings of nitrate of potash may be applied once a month at the rate of 1 oz. per 2 yds. of row, or failing this a mixture of sulphate of ammonia and sulphate of potash, each $\frac{1}{2}$ oz., may be successfully used. Leeks should be lifted as required during the winter.

EARLY PEAS.—If the war-time gardener has a heated pit or a frost-proof greenhouse at his command, there is no reason why he should not make a sowing under glass in the first or second week of February, because this would yield an extra early crop of peas. If this idea is adopted two seeds should be sown together 1 in. deep and 4 in. apart in soil-filled boxes. The seedlings, after hardening-off, are ready for planting out in the open in early spring.

A quarter of a pint of seed is required for the 42-ft. row of the 90 ft. by 60 ft. allotment or garden plot, so if very early peas are to be grown it might be advisable to sow $\frac{1}{8}$ pint ; that is, sufficient for half a row. The other half of the row and the second row could then be sown for the usual early crop.

Two Sowings for a Succession.—Whether the full two rows or one and a half rows are to be sown with early peas, it is advisable to make two separate sowings at an interval of two weeks. The cropping season of peas is not a very long one, so this double sowing prolongs it. The half-row might well be sown first—using $\frac{1}{8}$ pint of seed—followed by the second row, using double the quantity of seed.

TO KEEP BIRDS AND MICE FROM YOUR PEAS

Sowing Pointers.—Peas should always be damped with paraffin and then rolled in red lead before being sown, since this keeps birds and mice at bay. The early peas should be sown in early March and again towards the end of March, the seeds being covered by 3 in. of soil if the soil is light, or 2 in. if the soil is heavy, while in both cases the seed should be spaced 3 in. apart.

Peas grow well in practically any kind of soil, provided it is not in the slightest degree sour. This suggests that the site should have been limed a year or two before. The ground for the early peas should be deeply dug by double digging and a full dressing of manure or an efficient manure substitute worked into the lower spit. Two excellent chemical mixtures for peas are kainit, 6 lb., and superphosphates, 3 lb., per rod ; or kainit, 2 lb., superphosphates, 3 lb., and sulphate of ammonia, $\frac{1}{2}$ lb., for the same area.

MAIN-CROP PEAS.—Again with the object of obtaining a long succession of pickings, the main-crop peas should not be sown all at once. A good plan is to sow the first row at the end of March, the second row at the end of April, and the third row at the end of May. One quarter of a pint of seed is required per row, but as this is just a shade on the liberal side it should be possible to make do with $\frac{5}{8}$ pint for the three rows, dividing it as equally as you can between them.

PREPARE EARLY FOR MAIN-CROP PEAS

TRENCHES FOR MAIN-CROP PEAS.—It means extra work, of course, but it is always worth while preparing special trenches for the main-crop peas. A trench should be opened for each row 15 in. in depth and 15 in. in width. The next spit of soil should be thoroughly broken up with the fork— peas are deep-rooting—and given a generous dressing of manure or manure substitute. Next should come 6 in. of good garden soil containing a goodly quantity of humus, together with a moderate amount of manure or decayed vegetable refuse. Then the trench should be filled with ordinary good garden soil.

These trenches should all be made a month before the seed is to be sown, but as a general rule it will be found better to make the three at the same time—towards the end of February. The idea of early preparation is that it gives time for the soil to settle and for the added plant food to become available.

When sowing day comes round the seed should be put in 3 in. deep and 3 in. apart—after rolling in red lead. If birds are likely to be troublesome, a network of black cotton should be made above the rows to keep the birds away.

Supporting Peas.—Peas grow to a considerable height, so ample room must be left between the rows, and the plants must be properly supported. Three feet between the rows is sufficient.

As soon as the seedlings attain a height of a couple of inches or so, small pieces of twigs should be inserted so that they are given a start on their climbing career. In addition, ordinary pea sticks—long twiggy sticks—should be inserted in the ground on each side of each row. These should be forced well in as they have a considerable weight to support later on.

Pea sticks do not cost a lot of money; in fact, they can usually be obtained locally at a cheap rate. All the same, they should be stored carefully after use so that they may be used year after year. Cut off any decayed parts and keep in the shed.

To Pick the Pods.—All pods as soon as they reach a usable size should be picked at once. This increases the productiveness of the plants because it relieves them of a certain amount of strain. In any case young peas are always more delicious than older ones. Never just tear off the pods—cut them off with scissors. Should it happen that there is a glut of pickable peas at any time do not leave them on the plants, but gather them as usual. You can bottle them easily.[1]

The same artificial manure mixture should be used for the main-crop peas as recommended for the early variety.

RUNNER BEANS.—Runner beans are very prolific, so two rows should be quite sufficient, while there may still be a proportion of the crop which can be bottled for winter use. The sowing season is rather later than in the case of peas. Two sowings should be made—one in May and the other in June.

Although it means extra work, runner beans should always be grown in specially prepared trenches, if bumper crops of good quality are to be achieved. The trenches should be got ready at the same time as those for the main-crop peas.

This is the way to go to work. For each row mark off a 2-ft. wide strip. Remove the top spit of soil and put it on one side. Fork over the second spit of soil and excavate it and place apart from the top soil. Then fork over the third spit, and when doing this work-in plenty of strawy manure or partly decayed vegetable refuse. Then you can rest on your

[1] See page 37

spade for a while—or use it for some other purpose—because the trench should be left in this state for two or three weeks.

The top and second spits of soil should be placed one on each side of the trench and their tops should be flattened and covered with a liberal dressing of manure or manure substitute. After the end of, say, three weeks, the two lots of soil should be returned to the trench in the order in which they were removed (the manure should be mixed with the soil during the process) and the surface left in a rough state until shortly before sowing. Part of the top soil should not be put in, however, since it is advisable to have the surface of the trench soil 4 in. below the level of the surrounding ground —this saves a great amount of water, since all the water applied goes directly to the roots of the plants.

The seed can be sown in a single line or in zigzag fashion. In the former case space the seeds 3 in. apart ; in the latter 5 in.

HOW TO SAVE SPACE FOR YOUR RUNNERS

To Dwarf Runner Beans.—Since the desire is to grow as many different crops as possible and because runner beans grow to a considerable height, it is suggested that they should be dwarfed. When the first climbing shoot attains a height of 9 in. to 12 in. the tip should be nipped off, and as other shoots make their appearance and reach the same height their tips should also be removed. This induces the plant to grow into a little bush.

It may be wondered why, when French beans are also recommended, the runners should be dwarfed in this way, since they are then more or less similar to the French sort. The reasons are that dwarfed runners are more prolific than French beans and they are not affected to the same extent during a prolonged dry period.

The best artificials to use for runner beans are superphosphates, 3 lb., kainit, 2 lb., and sulphate of ammonia, 1 lb., per rod, while weekly doses of liquid manure should be given as soon as the pods begin to form.

SHALLOTS.—Pickles are likely to be used more largely in war-time than in normal times, so it is suggested that a row of shallots should be grown. Home-pickled shallots are really excellent, provided the " true " shallot is cultivated. The " true " shallot is not very large, just about the size of a walnut. See that you buy these—1 lb. is plenty for the one row—and no others.

The soil should be fairly rich, but certainly not freshly

manured. A dressing of soot proves particularly beneficial, however, so this should not be omitted.

What shallots do require is a well-firmed soil, so if you have a light garden roller use this before planting ; if not, tread the soil thoroughly unless it happens to be very heavy indeed. Press the bulbs into the soil, so that their tips are just visible, spacing them 6 in. apart. Shallots should be planted directly into the soil, any time between February and July. An excellent variety is Ryder's Giant.

Round about the early part of July, when the shallots should be fully grown, draw the soil away from the bulbs so that they are exposed to the air and sunshine. Afterwards, when the tops die down, lift, place in a sieve, and remove the soil by vigorous shaking. Then spread them out on the floor of the shed, or elsewhere under cover, until properly ripened. To store—unless they are pickled straight away—put them into a string bag and hang them in a cool, dry room or cellar.

HOW TO BOTTLE PEAS AND BEANS

Many home-grown vegetables can be dried or bottled. It is not suggested that any should be dried, for two reasons. There are certain to be plenty of dried vegetables on the market which can be bought at a reasonable price and, if the cropping plan advised is adopted, there should be no scarcity of fresh vegetables throughout the winter.

The idea of bottling peas and beans may, however, commend itself to the war-time gardener, because they afford a very welcome treat when the family is beginning to tire of cabbages, cauliflowers, and the like.

Bottling the surplus peas and runner and dwarf French beans is a good proposition, but as proper bottles have to be purchased (jam jars and the like are not really satisfactory) the cost may be considered excessive. But the proper bottles —glass ones, fitted with glass tops and rubber bands—last for years when looked after carefully.

To bottle, take tender, not quite fully-grown beans, and cut them into pieces, while the young peas should be shelled. Place them into a little salted water and boil for two or three minutes. Add a sprig of mint in the case of peas. Cool under running water. Boil some water with a pinch of salt and a little sugar. Pack the beans or peas closely into the bottles, fill with the prepared water, place into a deep pan on a wooden stand so that the liquid comes right up to the rims, and boil for an hour and three-quarters. After boiling fill up with more boiling water and cap immediately.

TO GROW BUMPER ROOT CROPS

THE various roots grow well in practically all ordinary soils, but while the soil should be fairly rich it should not be freshly manured. The one exception is in the case of potatoes, and for this crop it is quite in order to apply a good dressing of animal manure or a manure substitute in the autumn. The ground should be quite good enough for carrots, parsnips, and onions, if the rotation of cropping suggested is adopted.

BEETROOTS.—In some households beetroots are eaten as a vegetable ; in others the roots are sliced and pickled. Those who like beets boiled and served as a vegetable are advised to make two or three separate sowings from April onwards at intervals of two or three weeks. For pickling beets the whole row should be sown in the first week of May. One ounce of seed is plenty for a 42-ft. row, and the depth of the drill should be 2 in. in light soil or 1 in. in heavy land. Later on the plants should be thinned to 4 in. or 5 in. apart.

The round variety of beet should be chosen if the soil is shallow ; the long variety if of sufficient depth, say, 2 ft. of good soil. The soil should be well worked whichever variety is chosen, and if on the poor side guano, 1 oz. per square yard, should be pricked into the surface just before sowing.

During the active growing period the beets may stand in need of a little stimulating food ; 1 oz. of sulphate of iron to the gallon of water should be applied, while four weeks later a little poultry manure should be sprinkled along the sides of the rows and pricked in.

Lifting and Storing Beetroots.—Beets should be lifted in the way suggested for carrots, but in this case it is particularly desirable that the soil be fairly dry so that the roots are not too dirty. When lifted the foliage should be twisted and not cut off. Cutting causes bleeding, with the result that the roots assume an anæmic colour. Beetroots should be stored in the same way as carrots.

A GARDEN FOOD RICH IN VITAMIN A

CARROTS.—A large number of carrots is not used in the average household, but all the same it is suggested that there should be two rows. These roots contain a substance known as carotin which produces vitamin A in the body and they are, therefore, particularly valuable in war-time. Carrots are in reality one of the protective foods and, at the same time, they are delicious when young or old and they can be used in various ways.

Carrots, unlike other vegetables, are not thinned once only. The idea is to pull the young roots as they are required. Young carrots form an appetising ingredient in green salads whether cut into dice or grated.

The site for the two rows of carrots should be deeply dug, and during the digging process 2 oz. of kainit per square yard should be incorporated, and 2 oz. of superphosphates for the same area should be worked into the top few inches of soil immediately before sowing. Wood ashes should also be scattered over the surface at the same time and lightly pricked into the soil.

If the allotment or garden plot does not boast a greenhouse the seed-bed can be enlarged and, since carrots are such a health-promoting food, a little carrot seed may be sown in a part of it during the second half of February to provide an early crop.

In any case one-half of a row might be sown in early March to give a fairly early crop, and the other row and a half in early April for the main-crop. One half ounce of seed is sufficient for each 42-ft. row.

The seed should be sown 1 in. deep on light soil and a quarter of an inch shallower on heavy soil, while there should be 1 ft. between the rows. The seeds are rather sticky, so to allow for thin sowing they should be mixed with a little dry earth.

What Carrots to Grow.—There are three different kinds of carrot—the shorthorn, the intermediate, and the long. If the soil is shallow the first-mentioned should be chosen ; if of medium depth the intermediate, and if deep then the long.

When thinning is completed the plants should stand 3 in. apart. At this time a dressing of soot is advised, a showery day being the best occasion to give it. If the soil is thought to be rather on the poor side, $\frac{1}{2}$ oz. of guano or poultry manure may be applied to the yard of row.

Lifting and Storing Carrots.—When the carrots are ready for lifting, the fork should be driven into the soil vertically some 5 in. from the roots and then pulled back so as to loosen the soil round the roots. No drying of the roots is necessary before they are placed into store.

After lifting, the tops should be cut off together with a small segment of the top of the roots. A cool, dark place should be selected for storing these and other roots. The best plan is to put down a little straw and cover with sand ; then the carrots may be arranged like the spokes of a wheel with their tops outwards ; then comes a layer of sand followed by more roots, more sand and so on, with the top layer sand. If sand is difficult to obtain, dry earth may be used.

ONIONS.—A fairly rich soil is necessary for onion-growing, but one which has been manured for a previous crop. Two essential foods, however, are wood ashes and soot. Immediately before sowing, these should be sprinkled liberally on the surface of the soil and pricked in with the fork.

The best time to sow is March, and ½ oz. of seed should prove sufficient for two rows. The seed should be sown from ¾ in. to 1 in. deep, according to whether the land is heavy or light, and the plants should eventually be thinned to 4 in. apart.

While freshly manured ground is unsuitable for onions, watering occasionally with liquid manure (horse, cow, pig, poultry, guano, soot and nitrate of soda) proves beneficial.

Ripening and Lifting Onions.—Round about the end of July the onions should be fully grown. This is the time to ripen them preparatory to lifting. Using the back of the rake, the foliage should be bent over so that it assumes a horizontal position. As soon as it is seen that the foliage has turned yellow the bulbs should be raised a little out of the soil—a hand-fork does this work well—for this continues the ripening process and makes for firmness and good keeping properties.

Two or three weeks afterwards the soil round the bulbs should be loosened and then lifting can proceed. In dry weather the onions should be left lying on the ground for a few days ; in wet weather they should be placed in boxes and dried at one of the shed windows.

The general-purpose shed is an excellent place for storing the onions. Stretch string netting under the roof and put the bulbs therein in a single layer ; in very cold weather cover with straw, sacking, matting, or other suitable material.

A ROOT VEGETABLE YOU CAN HARVEST AS REQUIRED

PARSNIPS.—When the condition of the soil and the weather permit, parsnips may be sown in the open towards the end of February, but in most districts early March is the selected time. For the single row ½ oz. of seed is ample, the drill being ½ in. to ¾ in. deep for light and heavy land respectively. Eventually the plants must be thinned to 9 in. apart.

If long, straight roots are to be grown, fresh manure must not be applied to the ground. If the soil is on the poor side, however, artificial manure may be used—2 parts of super-phosphates and ½ part of sulphate of potash is a good mixture to apply before sowing, using 1 oz. per yard of row.

Parsnips are not usually lifted and stored in the same way

as other root vegetables. When the ground can be spared, the roots should be left in the soil—they are greatly improved after being touched by the frost—and lifted as required. When the site is wanted later on, they should be lifted and stored as suggested for carrots.

POTATOES : THE GARDEN'S MOST IMPORTANT CROP

POTATOES.—A common way of planting potatoes is to open a trench, put down some animal manure, place the tubers on top and cover with soil. This is altogether the wrong way of going to work, since it results in the production of far too much top growth and small tubers. If the land requires it a full dressing of animal manure may be applied in the autumn and, failing this, a mixture of chemicals should be used. One which can be recommended is superphosphates, 2 lb., and sulphate of ammonia and sulphate of potash, each ½ lb. After the trench has been opened this mixture should be thinly scattered and covered with a little soil.

Choice of " Sets."—The best potatoes for planting are those which weigh round about 2 oz. each and are of the size of an average hen's egg. On the average there are seven to the 1 lb., so 6 lb. is ample for the 42-ft. row. If there is a scarcity of suitable tubers they may be cut and the cuts liberally powdered with a mixture of sulphur and lime. This is not advised, however, if it is possible to avoid it.

Early potatoes are always acceptable, so it is a good plan to have two rows of them. One row may be planted at the beginning of March and the second during the first week of April ; or both rows may be dealt with at the same time, towards the end of March.

It is advisable to sprout tubers for both the earlies and the second early potatoes before planting. The selected tubers are placed into shallow trays some weeks before planting is due and kept in a frost-proof shed or room of the house. December—towards the end of the month—is a suitable time to start sprouting.

On light soil the tubers should be planted 6 in. deep, on medium soil, 5 in., and on heavy soil, 4 in. They should be spaced 1 ft. apart and there should be 2 ft. between the rows.

The Main-crop Potatoes.—The tubers for the main-crop— seven rows are advised—should be planted in the same way, but they should not be sprouted. The best time to plant is about the middle of April, but a good deal depends upon the weather and the state of the soil.

With both crops of potato earthing-up is an essential task, the principal objects being to protect the tubers and to prevent them turning green (and so becoming unusable) owing to the action of the light. Earthing-up should be done twice, and on each occasion a little soil should be drawn up on each side. The soil should not come to a point, but a V-shaped depression should be left at the stems, this forming a trap for any water which runs down from the foliage.

Before the first earthing-up, if it is known that the soil is rather deficient in plant food, a little chemical manure should be applied to the soil to be drawn up. An excellent one consists of kainit, 3½ lb., sulphate of iron, 1 lb., and superphosphates, 7 lb., per rod.

Lifting, Grading, and Storing.—If the season is a wet one it is advisable to cut down the haulm quite close to the ground some days before the potatoes are to be lifted. This gives the ground a better chance to dry and so lifting is made an easier job.

HOW TO LIFT POTATOES

The best implement to use for lifting is a flat-pronged fork, because it is not so liable to damage the tubers. The fork should be driven into the soil about 9 in. away from the stems of the plant in a vertical direction for half its length, and then turned so that it gets well beneath the plants. Lift each plant and throw forward and at the same time give it a shaking. If this method of lifting is adopted very few tubers remain in the ground.

Early potatoes should be dug as required, but all the main-crop should be lifted at the same time. The main-crop tubers should be exposed to the light and air so that the skins set—a matter of only a few hours in fine weather.

The tubers vary considerably in size, while some of them may be slightly affected by disease. Sorting and grading suggest themselves. All damaged tubers and any which are slightly diseased should be placed on one side for immediate use, and any which are badly diseased should be burned out-of-hand. The remainder of the tubers should be divided into two lots—those which are large enough to warrant storing and those which are small and only suitable for feeding to the poultry. Most potato diseases are of fungoid origin, so the haulm should be burned.

Since only sound potatoes are to be stored, the easiest and simplest method is to place them into boxes holding, say, a couple of hundredweights each, and fitted with lids or covered with straw. They can, however, be stored in a dark cellar—laid on a bed of straw and covered with the same material.

To be on the safe side give an occasional sprinkling with lime and sulphur as the tubers are being packed in the boxes or the heap made up on the shed or cellar floor.

QUICK-GROWING CATCH-CROPS

SINCE the object of war-time gardening is to make the best possible use of every square foot of ground, some unusual suggestions are given here for catch-crops and follow-on crops.

It is exceedingly difficult to make definite plans for catch-cropping, since a lot depends upon the way in which the major crops are growing and whether the weather is favourable for sowing when the various catch-crop subjects should go in.

The war-time gardener should take every advantage of growing quick-maturing crops between rows of slower-maturing ones. Various ways and means of doing this will suggest themselves to the individual gardener, but certain general directions can be followed to advantage.

Nothing is said regarding the soil for these crops, since it will already have been prepared according to the requirements of the slower-growing or maturing crop. If the directions given are carried out, really first-class crops should be forthcoming.

The following are all suitable subjects for catch-crops :

CARROTS.—One row of carrots may be sown beside the autumn cauliflowers in place of one row of turnips, if preferred. These carrots should be used while still quite small. A shorthorn variety should be chosen, sown in the same way as the other carrots and about the middle of March.

SALAD ONIONS.—Green salads are always in demand, particularly during the spring, summer, and autumn, and the vast majority of people like an onion flavour added in the way of " spring " onions. While the thinnings may be used for the purpose, it is better to grow a genuine salad variety of onion. Plenty of room can be found between the rows of cabbages and cauliflower for raising a large number.

Early March—towards the end of February if the season is an advanced one—is a good time to sow the seed, of which $\frac{1}{4}$ oz. is required per row of 42 ft.

LETTUCE, RADISHES, AND CRESS

OTHER QUICK-GROWING SALADINGS.—Other saladings—lettuce, radishes, mustard and cress—should all be sown at two-week intervals from the beginning of March to the end of August, between slower-maturing crops, as opportunity permits. A quarter of an ounce of lettuce seed is plenty for one row, the plants being thinned to 9 in. apart. Cabbage lettuce (the round variety) is easier to grow than cos lettuce (the long) and is therefore recommended.

Radishes are ready for picking—they should never be allowed to remain in the ground so long that they become stringy—in about three weeks, and ½ oz. of seed is necessary per row. Part of a row only should be sown at a time, because a large number is not usually wanted.

Mustard and cress take only a few days to attain the right height for eating, so in this case the idea of making a small sowing of each once a week may appeal. A couple of ounces of seed should see the average gardener through the whole season.

SUMMER SPINACH.—A suitable place for summer spinach is between the rows of brussels sprouts, but other sites do equally well. Summer spinach should be sown from March to June in drills 1 in. or ½ in. deep, according to whether the soil is heavy or light. The plants should stand 4 in. to 6 in. apart after thinning.

TURNIPS.—When turnips are wanted for putting with other " pot herbs " into the water in which a sheep's head is being cooked, or when they are required for making vegetable broth, the small-holder should suggest to the one in charge of the kitchen that they should be bought. The only turnips which are worth eating as a vegetable are young ones about the size of a tennis ball—or slightly smaller. The larger roots require more space than the average-sized garden can afford. Good varieties to choose are Early White, Early Milan, Golden Ball, and Red Globe.

An excellent place for turnips is on each side of the row of autumn cauliflowers, but other sites of a similar nature may also be available.

Sow thinly about mid-March—½ oz. of seed should prove sufficient—and thin out at a later date to 4 in. between the roots. Two rows should yield about 250 small roots.

The roots should be pulled as required for household use.

FOLLOW-ON CROPS

THE follow-on crops are sown in the autumn as the sites become available, or at a rather earlier date in the seed-bed, in order to have the young plants ready for planting out at the right time.

BROAD BEANS.—Although it is a little unusual, it is suggested that the best time to sow this crop is about the middle of October as a follow-on crop in some vacant space on the first vegetable plot. The advantages of an autumn sowing of broad beans are that the crop is an early one and the plants are practically immune from black fly.

The site should be forked rather deeply and the surface

reduced to a fine tilth. Then a trench 1 ft. wide and 6 in. deep
should be opened (1½ ft. between the trenches if more than
one row is to be sown) and the seed sown in zigzag fashion
and covered with 2 in. of soil. If the garden or allotment is
infested with slugs, occasional dustings with a mixture of
equal parts of lime and soot will usually be sufficient to keep
them away from your beans.

In very severe weather the young plants should be protected by covering with straw, this being removed as soon as
the need for its use is past.

An occasional watering with a solution of 1 oz. of sulphate
of iron to the gallon of water is recommended as a stimulant
during the active growing period.

SPRING CABBAGES.—The potatoes are all lifted about
the same time, so spring cabbage seed should be sown in
July in the seed-bed.[1] The plants can be put in at any time
from the middle to the end of October, being spaced 9 in.
apart.

If you keep fowls and rabbits they will consume plenty of
cabbages and other kinds of " greens," so full advantage of
the vacant potato plot should be taken.

WINTER LETTUCE.—Lettuces should be grown as a catch-
crop, but it is also useful to sow two or three rows in the seed-
bed towards the end of August for planting out in October—
8 in. apart—on the site recently occupied by the beets and
onions. A winter variety, such as Supreme or New York
Giant, should be chosen.

ONIONS.—Although plans are laid for growing onions for
storing during the winter and for sowing salad onions as a
catch-crop, the war-time gardener is strongly advised to make
a further sowing in August somewhere on his third vegetable
plot. The seed should be broadcast, but rather thinly. If it
is necessary to delay sowing until September it does not
matter.

This follow-on crop of onions is excellent, for it can be
used in two ways. The thinnings can be used during the
autumn, winter, and spring for salads, while the bulbs which
remain grow into an enormous size by the time the ordinary
onion crop is ready for lifting.

PRICKLY SPINACH.—If all the ground occupied by the
beetroots and onions is not wanted for winter lettuce, one or
two rows of prickly spinach may be sown, ½ oz. of seed being
required per row. The drills can be spaced 6 in. apart and,
when the time arrives for thinning, the plants should be left
so that they stand 6 in. from each other.

[1] See page 19.

THE HERB BED

IN the layout recommended,[1] a 4-ft. wide bed is set on one
side for herbs at the north end of plot 3.

The herb bed needs to be deeply dug, particularly that
section of it devoted to the perennial sorts which should be
allowed to remain undisturbed in the ground. If the soil is
in good heart, no munure is required, but if of poor quality
a little decayed vegetable refuse worked into the top spit may
be recommended. Plant mint in a damp, shady corner, and
on no account allow the roots to come in contact with wood
ashes. Cut stalks to the ground in the late autumn.

Herbs are divided into two main classes : annual and
biennial kinds which are raised each year by sowing seed,
and the perennials which are propagated by dividing the
roots. The annual and biennial herbs should be sown thinly
in drills in the spring. They include aniseed, basil, borage,
caraway, chervil, dill, purslane, rosemary, and summer savory.

The perennial herbs, which are permanent, comprise balm,
mint, chamomile, fennel, horehound, marjoram, sage, winter
savory, sorrel, tansy, tarragon, thyme and peppermint.

In July most of the herbs will be on the point of opening
their first flowers. It is at this time the majority of them
should be gathered if they are to be dried and stored for winter
use. A dry day should be chosen for the work, and all cutting
should be done with a sharp knife. Long stems should be
taken, tied into bundles and hung up in a cool, airy place for
slow drying. Sappy subjects, such as mint, should be tied into
smaller bundles than the drier kinds, such as thyme. When
the leaves are quite dry they should be rubbed off the stalks
and stored in air-tight fruit bottles.

OTHER VEGETABLES WORTH GROWING

So far details have been given of the vegetables every one will
want to grow and which, in any case, it is essential to cultivate
in war-time. The beginner is advised to concentrate first on
cabbages, potatoes, peas, etc., but gardeners with more
experience may consider it worth while to add a few of the
less usual vegetables to their war-time programme. In this
category also are included plants such as marrows and rhubarb.
These require a considerable amount of room and the provision of special hot-beds. They are not therefore suitable for
starting in a small garden or allotment at a time of emergency,

[1] See pages 2 and 3.

although, if space is available and the beds already in existence, they are well worth cultivating.

AMERICAN CRESS.—This is similar in flavour to watercress but much more easy to grow, for, while it appreciates a moist position, running water is not necessary. Sowings for succession may be made from March onwards until September.

Drills should be drawn ½ in. deep and 9 in. apart, and the seed covered lightly. The drills should be watered before sowing, and it is essential to keep the ground uniformly moist. As a second crop of leaves is produced after the first has been gathered, the plants should not be uprooted until this aftermath crop is over.

ARTICHOKES.—There are three kinds of artichoke—the globe, Jerusalem and the Chinese—but only the first two are usually grown. Globe artichokes may be raised from suckers or by root division, and both suckers and divided roots can be purchased; sowing seed is not altogether a satisfactory method.

A rich and rather moist soil is preferred. The roots or rooted suckers should be planted 4 ft. apart if in rows, but as a rule they are grown in isolated places, such as the corners of the main vegetable plots.

Jerusalem artichokes are excellent during the winter. The " sets " should be planted in February or March, allowing 15 in. between them. They require practically no attention afterwards, but when the plants are about 1 ft. high a little soil should be drawn up round the stems in the same way as potatoes are earthed-up. The plants grow to a considerable height and form an excellent windbreak.

A LITTLE-KNOWN BUT USEFUL ROOT

CARDOON.—This is an unusual vegetable of the artichoke type, but one which deserves to be grown more largely. The seeds should be sown towards the end of April. The best plan is to put in three or four together with 18 in. between the little bunches. When the seedlings are large enough to handle, thin them out to leave one only in each group.

As the plants grow they should be staked, and blanching should start in August. This is done by drawing the leaves together and wrapping them round closely with hay or straw bands and then heaping the soil all round. Blanching takes about eight weeks. Cardoons can be eaten as a vegetable boiled in the same way as artichokes. They are also very useful for flavouring soups and stews.

CELERIAC.—Neglected for many years, celeriac is fast

gaining in popularity. A sowing should be made in moderate heat in late March, if really large roots are to be obtained, and the young seedlings should be pricked-off into boxes as soon as they can be handled safely. Sow thinly, cover with the minimum of finely sifted soil and keep the box shaded until the seedlings make their appearance.

Celeriac thrives in the same conditions as celery, but no trench is required. The roots can be stored during the winter or even left in the ground in the South of England.

FOR YOUR WINTER AND SPRING SALADS

CHICORY.—One of the best winter and spring saladings is chicory. The seed should be sown in June in drills 1 ft. apart, and as the plants grow they should be thinned to 9 in. apart. As winter approaches the roots should be lifted carefully, planted in boxes in moist soil (deep boxes should be used) and placed in a shed or room in moderate warmth. A few roots should be put in at intervals of two or three weeks in order to ensure a continuous supply.

CHOU DE BURGHLEY.—This is a composite vegetable, for it is in reality half-cabbage and half-broccoli. The seed should be thinly sown in spring and the cabbage-like plant cut in the autumn or winter ; if the plants are left, broccoli-like hearts are formed. This plant is rather delicate, so the heads should be protected with paper or straw at the approach of winter.

EGYPTIAN ONIONS.—These are something of a novelty, but produce an excellent crop. The bulbs are planted in the same way as shallots, but clusters of onions are borne at the ends of upspringing stems.

ENDIVE.—This is a good vegetable to grow, for it takes the place of lettuce during the winter. The seed should be sown thinly in drills 12 in. apart in succession from the beginning of June to the end of August. As the plants develop they should be thinned to 12 in. apart.

Endive must be blanched before it is used. The plants should be tied up in the same way as cos lettuce by means of raffia, or they may be covered with pots or boxes. Only a few plants should be dealt with at a time so that supplies are available throughout the winter.

HARICOT BEANS.—This special type of bean should be sown and treated in the same way as runner beans. The beans can be gathered when green and cooked in the pod, or the pods may be allowed to ripen and the beans stored for use in winter. The pods are yellow when fully ripened.

A VEGETABLE FOR COOKING OR SALADS

HEADING CHINESE CABBAGE.—Those who live in a mild part of the country may grow heading Chinese cabbage or *Pe-tsai*, as it is known in its home country. It is a useful subject, because it may be used as a salading or as a vegetable. If wanted during the winter the seed should not be sown until July, since it runs to seed very quickly.

This cabbage needs a sheltered position and does best in light soil. When planted out, the seedlings should stand about a foot apart.

KOHL-RABI.—This is a particularly delicious vegetable, because it combines the qualities of the cabbage and the turnip, but yet possesses a flavour all its own. It should be sown in early April in the same way as the members of the cabbage family and transplanted when the seedlings are large enough. Place with 9 in. between the plants, in rows 1 ft. apart. The roots may be left in the ground throughout the winter or stored in a cool shed if more convenient.

MELONS.—Melons as grown in the heated greenhouse are luxury fruits for which no place can be found on the war-time allotment, but if you have a cold frame to spare there is no reason why you should not produce some of this delicious and health-giving fruit during the summer.

To prepare the ground beneath the frame, place a 3-in. layer of cinders, clinkers, broken bricks or small stones over the soil. Cover with a thick layer of leaf mould or manure (horse manure is the best, if you can get it) then with a 6-in. layer of garden soil sifted and mixed with equal parts of sand and liquid manure. Press down firmly, rake over and keep the bed slightly higher at the back than the front.

Sow (in March) each melon seed in a little pot of moist loamy soil, then bury the pots in the hot bed up to the rim. When the seedlings have taken root, transplant them to a mound of soil in the centre of the frame, selecting only the strongest. Allow 4 by 6 ft. of space for each seedling.

When the seedlings have grown 6 in. high pinch off the tops. Pinch off the side shoots when they are ten inches long. Do not allow surplus growths to form, but when the shoots show enough fruit, pinch out above the first or second leaf. Keep the frames warm and well ventilated, lifting the lights slightly when the weather is fine. Be sure to close them immediately the sun leaves the frames. Spray lightly with tepid water occasionally. The first melons are sometimes ready for cutting by the end of August, but September and October are the normal harvesting months.

PORTUGAL CABBAGE.—Portugal cabbage or *couve tronchuda* is an excellent substitute for seakale, which itself requires too much attention and space to be suitable for war-time cultivation. The seed should be sown in the seed-bed in May and the young plants put out in June. The older leaves are picked off and their midribs cooked and used in exactly the same way as seakale.

PURSLANE.—This is a very useful and easy crop to grow. It can be used in three different ways. It may be cooked, for the succulent leaves are delicious when treated in this way, but it may also be used in salads and when pickled it is particularly good.

Sow thinly in rich soil in May, in rows 6 in. apart. The growing plants should also stand 6 in. from one another. Purslane likes a dry, sunny position.

RAMPION.—This is another vegetable which may be used in more than one way. Its long creamy-white roots may be boiled or eaten raw in salads, while the leaves make an excellent addition to a green salad. Sow throughout the spring and thin as necessary to leave the plants about 8 in. apart. This plant does well in a fairly shaded position. The roots must be lifted and stored during the winter when not all used.

A TWO-PURPOSE CABBAGE

RED CABBAGE.—This is one of the best of all the pickling vegetables that can be grown, while it is also excellent when cooked as ordinary cabbage. The hearts grow to a very large size and are exceedingly easy to pickle. Sow in the seed-bed towards the end of March or the beginning of April and plant out as space becomes vacant. If large heads and firm hearts are desired, allow each plant plenty of room. Buy a very small packet of seed, because at most only half a dozen or so heads will be required.

RHUBARB.—Rhubarb is very easy to grow and bears a large number of sticks to one crown. It is a mistake, however, to put it in any odd corner, neglect it, and expect good results. Thin flabby sticks have little nutritive value and are not worth the space they occupy.

Plants may be raised from seed sown in heat in March and transplanted into the open in June. A better plan, however, is to buy crowns and plant in February. Increase is by division of the existing crowns when a new bed is being made from an old one.

Trench the site and manure heavily two or three weeks before planting ; plant 3 ft. apart in rows 4 ft. asunder. Some of the rhubarb plants should be forced. If a greenhouse is available lift some of the crowns and set under the staging in a bed of leaf-mould or old potting soil ; failing this, leave the crowns in the bed, cover with a large bottomless box with a movable lid, and surround the box with fresh stable litter and oak and beech leaves. When pulling is finished apply liberal quantities of liquid manure, and each fortnight for six weeks give ¾ oz. each of sulphate of ammonia and sulphate of iron to the gallon of water.

A FAVOURITE SUBSTITUTE FOR GARLIC

ROCAMBOLE.—Not many people care for the flavour of garlic, and for that reason it is not recommended for the war-time garden. Rocambole does appeal to quite a large number of palates, however, because it is a mixture of onion and garlic in flavour. It is a near relation of both, and responds to the treatment recommended for shallots.

SALSIFY AND SCORZONERA.—These two vegetables are grown and used in exactly the same way, so they may be considered together. The ground should be well trenched and the manure or manure substitute put into the second spit of soil. The site should be prepared in good time, and towards the end of March the rows should be forked over and a good tilth obtained.

The seeds should be sown in drills 1 in. deep with 15 in. between the rows. As soon as the seedlings are large enough to handle, they should be thinned to 12 in. apart.

In the autumn a part of the crop should be lifted and stored in sand in the same way as carrots and beets ; the rest should be left in the ground and lifted as required like parsnips. If the ground is wanted for any other crop the whole may be lifted and stored.

SEAKALE BEET.—Very rich soil is necessary for the successful cultivation of seakale beet or silver beet as it is sometimes called. It is a good supplement to spinach beet. It has a thick fleshy midrib which is delicious in flavour. This vegetable grows to a considerable size, so plenty of space must be allowed between the plants—1 ft. between individual plants and 18 in. between the rows.

Frequent watering in dry weather is necessary if the plants are to produce 2-in. to 3-in. wide midribs. The seed should be steeped in water for a day and a night before sowing. This hastens germination.

SPINACH BEET.—For an autumn supply, spinach beet, usually known as perpetual spinach, should be sown in late March. The best way to sow is to put a couple of seeds at intervals of 1 ft. in drills 15 in. apart. When the seedlings are large enough to handle the smaller and weaker one should be removed, leaving the other to come to maturity.

PEAS WITH EDIBLE PODS

SUGAR PEAS.—This special kind of pea is grown in exactly the same manner as recommended for ordinary peas, but it differs in that the pods are not only edible, but are succulent and possess a delicious flavour. The pods must, of course, be picked when young when they are at their best. As a change from ordinary peas they are universally appreciated.

SWEDES.—Garden swedes are quite distinct from the variety grown on farms and used for cattle and sheep feeding. They are after the nature of the turnip, but their flavour is somewhat different and some people prefer them to turnips, although this preference is not by any means general. Their value as food is much higher than that of the turnip.

Sown at the same time as turnips in the spring, or a little later, if the weather is cold, they are allowed to grow to maturity. They will grow on almost any soil and should be thinned to stand 1 ft. apart. They are easily stored and are available throughout the winter.

TURNIPS.—Turnips to be grown as a catch-crop and used when young have been already described.[1] If it is desired to grow full-sized roots, a little seed of a quick-growing variety such as Early White, should be sown, in a heated frame, in February, with a second sowing in March in the same way. Sowing outdoors should begin towards the end of March and continue at three-week intervals to August. Do not sow the seed deeply. When thinning is completed give a dressing of soot ; three weeks later give $\frac{1}{2}$ oz. of poultry manure or guano per yard of row. The plants should be thinned to stand four inches apart and thinned again later to leave the roots which are to mature 8 in. apart. The leaves which appear in spring can be used as a green vegetable—turnip tops.

MARROWS FOR COOKING AND PRESERVING

VEGETABLE MARROWS.—The usual idea is that vegetable marrows can be grown anywhere, even on a rubbish heap, but this is quite wrong. If really good fruits are to be obtained careful preparation of the site is necessary, and since this implies making a hot-bed of manure and leaves it is doubtful whether their cultivation in war-time is advisable or not. When the necessary materials can be obtained, however, there is no doubt that small marrows, weighing round about 1 lb., are delicious as a vegetable, while some of the fruits can be

[1] See page 44.

allowed to grow on into huge specimens and made into delicious preserves, such as marrow jam, marrow ginger, or pickled marrow.

A trench should be opened if more than one plant is to be grown, or a hole measuring 3 ft. square and 1 ft. deep. opened for an individual plant (one should be sufficient in most households). This should be filled with a mixture of leaves and stable manure and well trodden down, and then covered with a few inches of good soil. One plant should be inserted in the centre.

It is advisable to buy the plants, because otherwise it means sowing in mild heat in April and planting out the seedlings in May.

As soon as a few fruits have " set " give a weekly watering with liquid manure. Cut the first fruits when small, not only because they are better for cooking, but so as to relieve the plants of strain. Only in this way can large marrows be grown for preserving.

WINDOW-BOX GARDENING

WINDOW and balcony decoration is usually restricted to flowering plants and creepers, but in war-time many people will desire to grow something which is edible and so increase the quantity of vegetables and saladings cultivated. Quite a lot can be done in the few window-boxes for which a position can be found on the sills of the average house while, if there is a balcony, even runner beans can be grown. Whatever plants are cultivated on the balcony, they must be planted or sown in suitable boxes or small tubs—the former for preference, since a longer side is adjacent to the framework, up which climbing plants must be trained.

Window-boxes must be made of stout, well-seasoned timber and, as far as possible, they should be the exact size of the sill ; that is, as regards length. The question of width is a different matter. The wider the box within reason the better, since this means that more plants can be sown. If possible, a width of 9 in. is suggested as being not only practical, but also affording a considerable amount of room. If the sills are less than this it need be no deterrent, for the boxes can be attached to the wooden window-frames by means of hooks and eyes or strips of metal. On a sill with a steep slope this may be necessary in any case.

Seven inches is about the correct depth for a window-box, but those used for runner beans on balconies should be as near as possible 18 in. deep.

TO CONSTRUCT A WINDOW-BOX

The timber used should not be less than 1 in. thick and plenty of nails should be driven in so that the risk of the wood warping is minimised. Wedge-shaped pieces of wood will be necessary to counteract the natural slope of the sills. Fitting such wedges is easier than attempting to make the bottoms slope at the right angle.

Drainage holes are essential. They can be made with a $\frac{1}{2}$-in. drill or, if this tool is not available and you have a coal-fire, a red-hot poker serves as well. The holes should be 4 in. apart and most of them should be towards the front, so that surplus moisture from excessive watering or rain is given a better chance to escape.

Some kind of wood preservative is necessary. The inside of the boxes is best treated with tar and the outside painted with three coats of a first-class lead paint.

FILLING THE BOXES

The boxes should have the drainage holes covered in the same way as seed-boxes and flower-pots—by means of a few pieces of broken crock. Next should come a layer of very coarse soil or, better still, moss, so that the danger of the holes getting blocked up is minimised.

As a general rule, ordinary garden soil from a flower-bed is used for filling the boxes. This is a mistake, however, since such soil is not particularly rich in plant food. It pays to buy a bushel or two of really good loam if finances permit. If you have an allotment as well as the window-boxes, take some of the allotment soil which was liberally manured during the autumn, since this is eminently suitable. If you live in a large town and have neither garden nor allotment to provide soil, you can procure it either from a nurseryman, if there is one in your district, or from an oil-shop. Each box should be filled with soil to within 1 in. of the rim. After leaving for a few days the soil settles down, so about 2 in. is left. This amount of space is required for watering and weeding. A short-handled hoe or an old kitchen spoon or fork can be used to keep the weeds down and the surface soil in a fine state of tilth. It is also useful for removing little stones.

WHAT TO GROW

The most suitable subjects for growing in the war-time window-boxes are the various saladings[1]—lettuces, radishes, mustard and cress, and salad onions, with runner beans for

[1] For details of cultivation see pages 43 and 46

the balcony. Parsley may be induced to grow in a shady box and so may mint if the soil is kept sufficiently damp.

Gardening in a window-box follows the same principles as gardening on a larger scale. Be careful not to give the plants too much water nor to water them too frequently, otherwise the soil will turn sour and the plants will die. On the other hand, the soil must not be allowed to get dry and powdery.

Just as in a large garden, the soil needs rest and food from time to time. It can be kept sweet by an occasional watering with lime-water or by sprinkling it now and again with crushed egg-shells. But even so, it will need renewing every few years. For this purpose the plants must be temporarily removed to pots or other boxes and the soil given a good dressing of manure or even re-mixed.

In frosty weather the plants should be protected with cloth or paper, and in the summer care must be taken to see they do not stand in a perpetual draught.

FRUIT TREES AND TOMATOES

THE war-time gardener is sure to wish to plant a number of fruit trees and will probably want to grow tomatoes as well. Fruit is an invaluable food, for besides other things it provides vitamin C when eaten raw, and naturally dessert varieties of the hard fruits will be chosen.

It may not be possible to carry out exactly the plan shown in Fig. 1, but the plan can still be taken as a guide to how to cultivate both hard and soft fruits without taking up too great an amount of space.

Hard fruit trees are grown in a variety of forms or shapes as follows :

THE STANDARD.—This has a straight stem of 5 ft. to 6 ft.

THE HALF-STANDARD.—This has a stem of about 4 ft.

THE BUSH.—This has branches arising from the base and trained to grow cup-shaped.

THE PYRAMID.—A central stem gives off branches all the way up.

THE CORDON.—This is a tree restricted to one, two, or three stems, these being trained to grow perpendicular, oblique or horizontal.

THE ESPALIER.—This has three or four branches arising from each side of a central system, and the branches are trained to grow horizontally or fan-shaped.

CORDONS AND ESPALIERS THE WISEST CHOICE

Since the least possible space should be devoted to growing fruit on the war-time allotment or garden plot, it is suggested that only cordons and espaliers should be planted. These crop very well indeed, though occupying little room. They must, of course, be supported, but there is no difficulty in arranging this.

If there is no boundary wall or fence on the north side of the plot, a wire fence can be erected between the corners of the different permanent buildings, and the fence can be covered with wire-netting. Against such a fence both cordons and espaliers can be trained successfully. Cordons are preferable because they can be planted 3 ft. apart in the case of single stem trees or 5 ft. apart if there are three stems, while espaliers should be put in 12 ft. apart, when trained fan-shaped.

Another position where hard fruits may be planted is at the north end of plots 1 and 2 (Fig. 1). If this is done, a three-strand wire fence must be erected—neither a difficult nor an expensive matter—over which to train the trees.

WHERE TO PLANT THE SOFT FRUITS

Some of the soft fruits may be trained to trellis or over pergolas, but others can only be grown in the form of bushes. Pergolas are best erected at the ends of the main paths. Blackberries, loganberries and raspberries can be made to climb, while currants and gooseberries are soft fruits which must be grown as bushes.

If you are following the layout shown in Fig 1, two places which suggest themselves for the climbers are the sections of trellis in front of the leaf-mould and compost heaps. A currant or gooseberry bush might also be planted in front of the climbers.

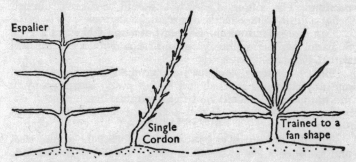

6. *Espalier and cordon fruit trees take up little space and, if no wall is available, can be trained against a wire fence which is easily constructed by the gardener. and is then covered with wire netting.*

If small bushes are grown, a few could be put in front of the espalier trees at the north end of plots 1 and 2. These bushes should be spaced 5 ft. apart.

CHOOSE HARD FRUITS THAT THRIVE IN YOUR DISTRICT

No attempt should be made to grow hard fruit if the land is chalky, because the cost of improvement would be too high. If the soil is light the addition of decayed leaves, pieces of old turf, old potting soil, and decayed vegetable refuse is advisable.

When choosing the kinds of hard fruit to be cultivated attention should be paid to the success or otherwise of different sorts in the district. For example, if it is known that apples or plums or pears do really well in the locality they should be chosen. Pears do not thrive well in all parts of the country, while plums are usually a failure in low-lying districts.

PLANTING THE YOUNG TREES

Fruit trees may be planted in the spring but, if possible, the work should be carried out during October and November, because this gives the young trees a chance of establishing themselves before the spring growing season. It is necessary, however, to await a favourable opportunity as regards weather conditions, so it may happen that planting must be postponed until December. No planting should be done if the soil is very wet, frozen hard, or covered with snow.

Young trees should be purchased and they must be planted at the same depth as they stood in the nursery garden. The necessary number of holes should be dug, and each should be large enough to accommodate the roots spread out in a natural position. The bottom of each hole should be slightly rounded being a little higher in the centre.

Manure is fatal to young trees, but wood ashes and a $\frac{1}{4}$ lb. of basic slag per square yard can be added to the top soil with advantage.

Before planting, each tree should be carefully examined and any damaged roots should be cut away, but as many of the fibrous roots should be left as possible.

ROOT-PRUNING

For the first three years it is better to lift the young trees and to prune a few of the thick roots. This work is best done in the autumn.

Cordons and espaliers do not require staking, since they are supported by a wire fence, but standards and half-standards, if these are chosen in preference to the others, should be staked when they are planted.

CARE OF THE TREE FRUITS

APPLES.—A well-drained, moderately heavy soil is best for apple trees, but there are varieties which will grow in practically any soil and in all parts of the country.

Pruning is a necessary task. March is the accepted time for pruning newly-planted trees. The leading shoots of espaliers should be cut back to within about 12 in. of the top pair of branches, and the other shoots (produced during the previous summer) should be shortened half-way. The side-shoots should be shortened to within two or three buds of the base. The leading branch or branches of cordons should be cut back just a little, but the side-shoots must be reduced to two or three buds. Standards, pyramids, and bushes should have the branches cut back two-thirds.

Established apple trees should all be pruned in summer, the side-shoots being cut back to five or six leaves, while as other shoots grow they should be cut back to the second leaf. In winter the side-shoots which were dealt with in the summer should be reduced to four buds—to three if the shoots are not very vigorous.

Established apples respond well to an application of liquid manure in late autumn, or, if this is not available, 1 lb. of kainit per tree in winter, or $\frac{1}{2}$ lb. of superphosphates and 1 oz. of nitrate of soda per tree in spring. Rather less should be used in the case of a single-stem cordon, say, one-half the quantity.

CHERRIES.—Cherries are not particularly suitable on the allotment or garden plot. The fruit has to be protected, so half-standard trees and bushes are preferable ; but if the boundary wall is of brick, as in the case of a garden, wall-trained trees may be planted, since they can be protected by hanging string-netting over the fruits.

The trees require little attention in the way of pruning when established, and young ones should not be pruned the first year. In the second winter the branches should be cut back one-half. This annual pruning is necessary for the first few years only ; afterwards nothing need be done save to cut out or shorten some of the branches to preserve the shape of the tree. Liquid manure should be applied in October.

DAMSONS.—Damsons are great favourites with many people but, if they are not already in the garden, they are not very suitable for planting in war-time. They thrive best when planted in the form of a hedge, and this occupies too much space in proportion to the produce it yields.

Damsons do excellently in practically all soils and in all parts of the country. Until the bushes are established, the shoots should be cut back one-third ; after-pruning consists of cutting out central shoots or branches so that light and air is allowed to enter the heart of the hedge. Manuring is unnecessary.

PEARS.—The best forms of pear trees are pyramids, cordons, and espaliers, so if the district is a suitable one for this fruit the two last-mentioned should be planted. The soil should be deeply dug, but no natural manure should be applied when planting the young trees. Pears should be lifted every year for three or four years as recommended in the case of apples. Manuring established trees and pruning are the same as for apples.

PLUMS.—Cordons and espaliers are not particularly good forms of plum tree, so it is possible this fruit will not be planted. If decided upon, however, a little turf and mortar rubble should be incorporated in the soil.

Newly planted trees should be cut back if necessary to make good branching heads. Little pruning in after years is needed save to thin the centre of the standard, half-standard or pyramid trees to keep them open. Summer pruning consists of cutting back the side-shoots to keep them within bounds.

Liquid manure should be applied during the summer, and each autumn 6 oz. of lime and 4 oz. of basic slag should be applied to each established tree.

The Value of Mulching.—Every autumn a mulch of old manure should be put down in the case of all established fruit trees and bushes, left on the surface during the winter, and be forked lightly into the soil in April or May.

TO GROW BERRIES AND TOMATOES

BLACKBERRIES.—As already mentioned, blackberries can be grown to produce an excellent crop when trained to trellis or to a pergola. The ground should be deeply dug and liberally manured before planting.

The ultimate aim should be to train the branches some 9 in. apart. In the spring, immediately after planting, the branches should be cut down practically to the level of the ground, for this induces the production of a number of new shoots which bear fruit the following year. In the case of established blackberries the only thing to be done is to cut out the old wood soon after the crop is over, training new shoots to take its place.

Apply a mulch of old manure in the summer and fork into the ground in the late autumn.

LOGANBERRIES.—This fruit is not at all particular as to soil, while it thrives splendidly in all parts of the country. It requires similar treatment to that described for blackberries.

RASPBERRIES.—While not climbers, raspberries have to be supported, usually by means of wires stretched between posts. If hard fruit trees are not planted at the north end of plots 1 and 2, as suggested in the layout,[1] the wire erected there may well be used for raspberries.

A rich, moist, deep soil is necessary for this fruit, so that trenching and liberal manuring are required. The canes should be planted 3 ft. apart in the autumn. Shortly after

[1] See pages 2 and 3.

planting, they should be cut down to within about 9 in. of the ground and mulched with rotted manure.

During the first spring only three shoots should be allowed to develop, the rest being cut out. As soon as the crop from the established canes has been gathered, the old canes should be cut out and five or seven of the young ones allowed to remain according to the strength of the plant.

An application of 4 oz. of basic slag per square yard in the autumn is recommended.

THE THREE CURRANTS.—Three different kinds of currant can be grown—the black, red and white. The first must be considered separately, because the treatment it requires differs from that called for in the case of the red and white.

The black currant does best in a cool, rich, moist soil. Young bushes should have the branches reduced to about 9 in. in the spring. Afterwards old branches should be cut out towards the end of the summer or early in the autumn so that plenty of space is left for the young ones which bear the fruit. Liberal applications of liquid manure should be made.

An ordinary garden soil does well for red and white currants, but it should be deeply dug and manured moderately. The currants are borne on spurs. Young bushes should be pruned as suggested for the black variety, but summer and winter pruning are also necessary when the bushes are established. All shoots, except those at the ends of the branches, should be reduced to the fifth or sixth leaf in July ; in winter these side-shoots should be cut back to the second bud from the base. Old branches should be cut out, as required, to provide space for young ones.

In the spring 2 oz. of superphosphates per square yard, together with 1 oz. of sulphate of ammonia, proves beneficial, while a mulch should be applied in the autumn and forked into the soil in the spring. Liberal waterings with liquid manure during the summer are helpful.

GOOSEBERRIES.—Gooseberry bushes not only crop well, but they require the minimum of attention. They thrive excellently in all ordinary soil, but deep digging and moderate manuring before planting are desirable.

Pruning is a simple business. Only superfluous branches should be cut out, a task that is best performed in February. When pruning is finished in the spring, a mulch of manure should be applied, and a dressing of 2 oz. of superphosphates per square yard is also beneficial when applied at the same time. Every third autumn 4 oz. of basic slag per square yard should be applied.

STRAWBERRIES.—Strawberries, delicious as they are, are

not suitable for growing in war-time in the small garden or allotment. A worth-while bed occupies a considerable amount of space and cultivation requires more time and attention than can be spared during war-time.

TOMATOES.—All the trusses of fruit on a properly stopped tomato plant do not ripen in the open in this climate, save in very favoured districts, but the later fruits can always be reddened by putting them in a sunny window. If the north boundary wall is a solid one it might be worth while raising or buying a few plants for planting in such a sunny position.

Raising the necessary plants is only possible when a heated frame or greenhouse is available. The average gardener has to buy them. They can be obtained at a very reasonable price ready for planting out in the open. The beginning to the middle of June is a good time to buy in most parts of the country.

A good loam is essential for successful culture. The plants should be spaced 18 in. apart, and for the first few nights they should be covered with flower-pots to afford them protection.

All side-shoots should be nipped off at their tips and any spray which does not exhibit signs of fruiting should be removed. When the plants attain a height of about 3 ft. the growing tip should be pinched out.

A weekly watering with weak liquid manure until the flowers make their appearance is recommended, while, when three trusses of fruit are formed, a mixture of superphosphates, $1\frac{1}{2}$ parts; sulphate of ammonia, 1 part; and sulphate of potash, $\frac{1}{2}$ part, should be very lightly sprinkled over the surface of the soil once a week and watered-in.

In order that the sun can reach the fruits the removal of over-shading leaves is a practical idea, but only those which actually obstruct the sun's rays should be cut off.

FLOWERS TO GROW IN WAR-TIME

A LARGE flower-garden at home or the devotion of a considerable proportion of the allotment plot to flowers is out of place in war-time, but this is no reason why quite a lot of flowers should not be grown, particularly those suitable for cutting. In fact, there are several excellent reasons why flowers should be cultivated in odd places in the allotment—between rows of very slowly maturing vegetables, for instance—and they can also be put in the narrow beds which usually surround the house.

Flower-growing, like every other branch of gardening, can be an exact science requiring a great deal of time and a considerable amount of more or less expensive equipment. On the other hand, reasonably satisfying results can be obtained from seeds costing a few pence and planted according to the instructions on the packet. A few experiments will soon show what flowers do well in your particular garden and which ones require more attention than you can afford to give.

If you had planned your garden or allotment as suggested, the soil to receive the flowers will have already been dug, manured, and prepared for vegetables. All you have to do for the flowers, therefore, is to select your sunny or shady spot according to the needs of the particular plants, and put in the seeds, roots, or cuttings at the right time of year. Suggestions are given here for flowers you will probably want to grow, together with fuller instructions for dealing with rather special plants such as sweet peas, perpetual carnations, and chrysanthemums.

TEN POINTS TO REMEMBER

The following general hints should be borne in mind :

1. If your flowers are to succeed, you must give them room to grow. Do not over-crowd the space available, therefore, by putting in too many different kinds of plants, and, when the seeds come up, thin them out to leave reasonable space between the seedlings.

2. If you want fine, large blooms, pick off some of the buds as they appear. This strengthens the two or three flower-heads you allow to remain.

3. If a clump of flowers such as pinks or carnations grow too large, dig up the root and divide it by cutting it into two or three with a spade. Then replant the pieces to make two or three smaller clumps.

4. If you have " green " fingers, you will probably have no difficulty in adding to the stock of your favourite flowers by taking cuttings. You will simply cut off healthy young slips, about 3 in. long, just below a joint. You will strip off the lower leaves, put the slips in the flower-bed or in a pot, and in due course find yourself with some thriving young plants.

If, however, your cuttings fail to root easily, you must take more care. Plant them in pots of sandy soil, putting the base of each cutting firmly on the bottom of its hole, and making the holes near the edge of the pot. Until the cuttings have rooted, keep them indoors, at a temperature of 50 degrees F., and put the pots in a glass-covered box. Lift the glass once a day and remove the moisture from the underside. Press the soil firmly round the base of each cutting and do not give too much water. If you are still unsuccessful, try leaving the slips to dry for a day before planting, and take cuttings of young shoots with a little of the old plant attached to them (heel-cuttings).

5. At all times of year keep your flower-beds free from weeds.

6. Do not imagine that you will get better results by a more liberal application of fertilizers and manures. Over-rich soil can be as harmful as poor soil, so in any experiments you make in this direction, go gently, and give too little rather than too much.

7. To keep the beds tidy and get the best results, see that the flower stems are not allowed to bend and break under the weight of the blossoms. In the case of flowers which you know will need support, put sticks in early, well before the time when their assistance is needed. For other plants, broken perhaps by a summer storm, put the sticks in and tie the stems to them as soon as you notice the damage.

8. Do not let dead blooms remain on the plants unless your particularly want their seeds. Otherwise nip the heads off as soon as they begin to fade.

9. In general, flower-beds should be kept well-picked during the flowering season, so do not hesitate to cut the blooms freely and frequently.

10. Flowers should be cut with scissors, secateurs or a sharp knife. They should not be plucked, since this damages the stems. The early morning is the best time for cutting.

THE THREE GROUPS OF FLOWERING PLANTS

There are three groups of flowering plants—the annuals, the biennials and the perennials. An annual is a plant which flowers the same year as the seed is sown and then dies. A biennial is one which flowers the season after the seed has been sown and then dies. A perennial is a plant which continues to grow year after year. Trees and shrubs naturally come under this heading.

While this classification is a correct one it is possible to grow annuals as biennials and some biennials as annuals. Here is an illustration. Hardy annuals (this does not apply to those annuals which are only half-hardy) are often sown in summer, the plants being carried through the winter in the open, and they produce flowers considerably earlier and for a longer period than those raised from spring-sown seed. It is possible to have biennials flowering the same year if the seed is sown under glass in January or February.

FLOWERS THAT DO NOT TAKE SPACE FROM VEGETABLES

The aim of the war-time gardener, so far as the production of flowers for cutting is concerned, is to secure a constant supply of blooms throughout the whole of the twelve months. Although this is not entirely possible, it is easy to arrange for suitable blooms for the greater part of the year, and this in addition to the vegetables and not at the expense of either their quantity or quality.

The places which can be used for flower-growing vary from year to year when a proper rotation of cropping is followed. For this reason it is suggested that for the most part reliance should be placed on the hardy annuals for the production of cut flowers. This does not mean going without flowers for six months of the year, because under ordinary conditions the various hardy annuals together provide blooms from June to October, while early ones can be obtained if some of them are treated as biennials, as already mentioned.

The remainder of the year can be filled in by growing a few special flowers in the open, such as perpetual border carnations and outdoor varieties of chrysanthemums, by growing bulbs in fibre and, if a greenhouse is available, raising perpetual flowering carnations (these are distinct from perpetual border carnations) and chrysanthemums.

Roses might well be grown ; possibly one or two bushes in the allotment (pillar roses are excellent at, say, each corner of the vegetable plots), while the garden at home should afford sufficient space for a few more. Climbing roses, too, might be used on the dwelling-house walls. Flowering creepers are also capital for training over the house walls, if the available space is not occupied by climbing roses.

THE HARDY ANNUALS TO CHOOSE

The vast majority of the hardy annuals do not attain a height of more than about 1 ft., with a few growing to 3 ft. Two of them—sweet peas and sunflowers—are considerably taller.

Many of the hardy annuals can be obtained bearing flowers of different colours, so the best way of suiting individual taste is to consult a nurseryman's catalogue. Choice can be made from any of the following hardy annuals : Alyssum, *calandrinis speciosa*, calendula (marigold), candytuft, annual chrysanthemum, clarkia, *collinsia bicoor*, cornflower, coreopsis, annual delphinium, dianthus (annual pinks), eschscholzia, gilia, godetia, *gypsophila elegans*, larkspur, limananthes, *linaria maroccana*, linum, love-lies-bleeding, lupin, malope, mignonette, nasturtium, nigella, poppy, silene, sunflower, sweet pea, sweet sultan, virginian stock and viscaria.

WHEN TO SOW HARDY ANNUALS

When treated as biennials the hardy annuals should be sown towards the end of August in a seed-bed. The vegetable seed-bed can be used splendidly for the purpose, the soil being in just about the right state and " heart." When they attain a suitable size the seedlings can either be replanted in another section of the seed-bed a few inches apart, there to remain during the winter, or, if the site is vacant, they can be put into their permanent flowering quarters. It is unlikely, however, that permanent quarters will be ready so early because this would interfere with the autumn digging—work which it is essential to do at the right time.

If spring sowing is decided upon, the best time is from the middle of March to the middle of April according to the weather conditions. In this case, the flowers should be sown where they are to bloom.

FLOWERS THAT COME UP YEAR AFTER YEAR

The biennials should be sown in the summer, in the way suggested for the hardy annuals ; the half-hardy varieties should be wintered in a frame, but the hardy ones can stand the normal winter out-of-doors with comparatively few losses. The roots can also be bought ready for planting, but this is more expensive and less interesting than growing from seed.

Some favourite biennials are Canterbury Bells, Forget-me-nots, Stocks, Sweet Williams, and Wallflowers.

Perennials are propagated from seeds, cuttings, offsets, layers and root division. Root division is the method adopted with the majority and, in the case of ordinary flowering garden subjects, the plants are usually lifted every second or third year according to the growth they have made, the roots divided, and the best pieces replanted.

Perennials are excellent for growing in war-time as they are inexpensive and require little attention once they have taken hold of the soil. On the other hand, they cannot be moved from place to place in the same way as annuals, and should only be put, therefore, in places where it is not desired to grow vegetables.

Hardy perennials which may be recommended are Antirrhinums (Snapdragons), Aquilegias, Arabis, Asters, Aubretia, Delphinium, Gaillardias, Geums, Michaelmas Daisies, Phlox, Primulas, and Violas. Choice can be made, however, from hundreds of others.

SPECIAL FAVOURITES FOR EVERY GARDEN

In addition to the usual annuals, biennials, and perennials, there are one or two special flowers which are not only first favourites but are also especially helpful in providing blooms when other flowers are unobtainable. Sweet peas, perpetual border carnations, and chrysanthemums are worth cultivating for this reason.

SWEET PEAS ARE EASY TO GROW

Sweet peas are popular flowers at all times but they are especially suitable for war-time cultivation. Easy to grow and requiring practically no special feeding, they provide a wealth of delightful flowers from June to September, in a large range of colours. Their one drawback is that they grow to a considerable height, from 4 ft. to 6 ft., so it may be rather difficult to find a suitable place for a row or two. Two spots, however, which might be chosen on an allotment arranged as suggested in Fig. 1 are the west sides of plots 2 and 3. Here the shade thrown by the plants would fall on the paths and not on any crop requiring plenty of sunshine to come to maturity.

TO SOW SWEET PEAS

Provided the district is not too exposed, it is possible to make a sowing of sweet peas in the late summer, but since space is at a premium and the selected sites may not be available, it may be found better to do the sowing some time in April as soon as the weather and soil conditions permit.

It is better to plant a short row of sweet peas and obtain a good crop of first-class blooms than a longer stretch with inferior flowers. With this end in view, the site should be specially prepared in early winter if this can be managed ; if not, later preparation, but at any rate a few weeks before sowing, is advised.

The row should be trenched and given a liberal dressing of animal manure or an efficient manure substitute (hop manure is excellent for this flower) in the third spit of soil as it is being forked up. After this should come 5 in. or 6 in. of unmanured soil, followed by the remainder of the second spit of soil with which has been mixed a good sprinkling of steamed bone-flour and superphosphates. Finally, the top spit should be returned to its original position, but without adding manure of any kind.

Shortly before sowing, the surface soil should be forked over and a little soot and lime scattered over it. The seed should be sown in drills some 3 in. apart and 1 in. deep. But when you buy the seeds ask whether the chosen variety should be " chipped " ; that is, have a little cut made through the hard skin on the side opposite the " eye." This is necessary in some cases ; it allows the moisture to get to the heart of the seed more quickly and so hastens germination.

Again with the idea of producing a comparatively limited number of really fine blooms, each plant should be restricted to one, two, or three stems according to the variety ; three is a suitable number with most sorts. If a profusion of not-quite-so-good flowers is required, each plant may be allowed to form as many stems as it likes.

Sweet peas should be supported in the same way as ordinary peas, although 3-in. or 4-in. mesh wire-netting serves the purpose well.

This flower does not require feeding in the accepted meaning of the word, but the colour of the blooms can be greatly improved if occasional doses of soot water are given.

PERPETUAL BORDER CARNATIONS

When perpetual border carnations are grown it is possible to have a succession of these delightful and ever-popular flowers for the greater part of the year, provided a greenhouse is available to carry the plants on through the winter.

Perpetual border carnations make pleasant edgings to the vegetable plots. They not only give colour to the allotment or garden, but also supply a wealth of particularly charming blooms for cutting.

Perpetual carnations are raised from cuttings which should be struck in very sandy soil in January, in a frame or greenhouse. The rooted cuttings can be kept in the open during the summer until about the end of August. The cuttings should be " stopped "[1] two or three times according to the needs of the variety.

The grown plants should be allowed to remain in the open as long as autumn weather conditions permit. They should then be lifted and potted and removed to the greenhouse, where they will continue to bloom for months. If there is no greenhouse, it is just possible that these plants will continue to produce flowers during the winter if placed in a room in the house, but in such a place they require careful management—the room must not be subject to too sudden changes in temperature—while the blooming period may be a little curtailed.

If you want really first-class blooms, remove the buds to leave only one to each stem. You will probably then find it necessary to give the stems some additional support, so that they do not break under the weight of the flowers.

CHRYSANTHEMUMS TO GROW OUTDOORS

The annual variety of chrysanthemums should certainly be grown, but each gardener must decide according to circumstances whether space can be given to the more permanent variety. If the cropping plan suggested is adopted it may be found that the garden is yielding more vegetables than the household can use. In this case, the necessary room can be freed for chrysanthemums.

Outdoor chrysanthemums can be increased in one of two ways—from cuttings in the summer or by the division of the root in the winter. If the war-time gardener decides to grow a few of these flowers, the site should be prepared some time in advance ; trenching, with the addition of a little old manure or thoroughly decayed vegetable refuse and wood ashes, is essential for the production of really good blooms.

If cuttings are struck in the summer they must be protected during the winter in the greenhouse or heated frame and, after hardening off, planted out in the open in May, so root division is a method of propagation which will probably recommend itself to most gardeners.

If it is decided to grow chrysanthemums, a careful study should be made of the nurseryman's catalogue. This will give details of the important operation known as " stopping " and

[1] See page 70.

will also explain the characteristics of those varieties which can be carried through the winter in the open.

"Stopping" is a process by which the growing tip of a young plant is pinched off with the object of checking over-hasty growth. "Stopping" sends the strength back into the main stems and results in a strong, bushy plant instead of a lanky one. How often a plant should be "stopped" and at what time depends on the particular variety.

INDOOR CHRYSANTHEMUMS FOR WINTER BLOOMS

To raise indoor chrysanthemums successfully involves a considerable amount of work, and not every war-time gardener will be able to afford time for them or have the necessary space to spare. But they are among the best plants for providing winter blooms and well repay the extra care they need.

If a succession of under-glass chrysanthemums is to be secured, cuttings should be struck between November and April. The best cuttings to take are the new shoots which arise round the base of the old plants. They should be from 2½ in. to 3 in. in length and cut off immediately below a joint. To obtain the necessary new shoots the old plants should be treated to a top-dressing of sifted loam and leaf-mould, this being put down to a depth of about half an inch.

For the cuttings use a compost consisting of ordinary soil, 3 parts; leaf-mould, 1 part; old mortar rubble, ½ part, and a decent sprinkling of bone-meal. Take a 3-in. pot and insert four cuttings round the edge.

The pots should be plunged to their rims in ashes and kept in a box closely covered with glass at a temperature of about 50 degrees F. For the first three or four days keep them covered, but open up once a day and wipe away any moisture which may have condensed on the underside of the glass. Admit more and more air afterwards, increasing the amount daily. The earliest cuttings usually take about five weeks to root; later ones about three weeks.

The rooted cuttings should be shifted singly into 3-in. pots, these containing a similar compost to that used on the first occasion, and placed in a frame close to the glass in a temperature of 50 degrees. When the pots are full of roots—in March with November cuttings—the plants should be re-potted, this time into 5-in. pots, an excellent compost being loam, 3 parts; leaf-mould, 1 part; well-rotted manure, 1 part; lime rubble, ½ part; and a liberal sprinkling of bone meal, sand and wood ashes.

Once more re-potting is necessary (about June in the case of the earliest cuttings), and for this, the final shift, 8-in. or

10-in. pots should be used. The greenhouse chrysanthemums are best kept in the open during the summer, and during this period they should be given weekly applications of weak soot water and weak liquid manure alternately, but the soot water can be replaced by a good chrysanthemum fertilizer after the end of the first month. " Stopping " should be done as indicated in the nurseryman's catalogue.[1]

Round about the early part of October the pots should be removed to the greenhouse and kept in a minimum temperature of 50 degrees F. Continue feeding with a good fertilizer until the buds are partly opened.

FIBRE-GROWN BULBS TO FLOWER INDOORS

A magnificent array and a long succession of delightful blooms for the house can be produced by growing bulbs in fibre. The war-time gardener will find it advantageous to grow many other bulbous plants besides the usual ones—hyacinths, daffodils, tulips and narcissi. Among those which lend themselves well to fibre-growing are bleeding heart, iris reticulata and Spanish irises, fritillary, crocus, scilla, freesia, aconite and grape hyacinth. A charming display can be obtained by planting a number of these bulbs all together in the same bowl.

The necessary bowls need not cost a lot of money, since composition ones are inexpensive. The fibre and charcoal will require a certain expenditure but less than would be used to buy cut flowers if no bulbs were grown. It is really better to purchase ready-prepared fibre, for it not only saves a lot of trouble, but it contains the necessary oyster-shell, charcoal and, in many cases, plant food of a chemical nature which is particularly suited to bulb requirements.

The fibre as bought should be placed in a sack and soaked in water for a couple of days—a bucket may be used if the quantity of fibre is not great—hung up to drain and then used at once. The fibre should be really moist through and through ; when a little is taken in the hand it should be possible to squeeze out a few drops of water.

A few pieces of charcoal should be placed in the bottom of each bowl ; this prevents the fibre going sour, a likely happening as no drainage holes are provided in the bowls. The charcoal should be covered with 2 in. to 3 in. of the moist fibre and the bulbs should be placed 1 in. apart all over the surface. Then more fibre should be used to within $\frac{1}{2}$ in. of the rim.

[1] See page 70.

After filling, the bowls are best kept in the garden shed or in some outhouse at home and allowed to remain there for five or six weeks, the idea being that roots are formed before top growth becomes evident. As soon as 1 in. of top growth has been made, place the bowls in a strong light and give them as much sun as possible until they flower. But turn the bowls round a bit each day, otherwise the stems will grow crooked —towards the light.

The one thing that is necessary is to keep the fibre in the bowls uniformly moist. As required, pour on water until it reaches the rim, leave for a while and then tilt the bowl so that the surplus water can drain out.

CREEPERS GIVE COLOUR TO YOUR WALLS

If suitable flowering creepers are selected for the decoration of the house walls and possibly the shed walls, the result is highly attractive, because they are in bloom from April to October. Most creepers like plenty of sun, but some, such as ivy, will grow in a shady position.

The site for creepers must be properly prepared, for they are perennials and are left undisturbed for a number of years. September is a good month for preparing the sites. To ensure adequate drainage, a few clinkers and some ashes should be mixed with the third spit of soil, strawy manure or a reliable manure substitute and a little old mortar with the second spit, while a moderate dressing of well-rotted manure should be incorporated with the top soil.

The best month for planting is October. Once the creepers are established, all they need is a mulch of manure or leaf-mould every spring or early summer. In general, only slight pruning is required, enough to keep the plants shapely and give new wood room to grow. Spring-flowering creepers should be pruned as soon as flowering is over. Autumn-flowering ones are pruned in winter or spring.

Excellent evergreen creepers are : *Akebia quinata, ampelopsis sempervirens, clematis armandi,* irish ivy (*hedera canariensis*) and *jasminum officinale.* Among the best leaf-losing creepers are *ampelopsis veitchii* (a Virginia creeper), *aristolochia sipho* (Dutch-man's pipe), *clematis flammula,* common hop, *hydrangea scandens,* honeysuckle, passion flower, and the three wistarias, *alba, chinensis* and *multijuga.*

When deciding what creepers to plant, the height of the house should be taken into consideration. For instance *ampelopsis veitchii* and *ivies* are suitable only for high walls.

HINTS FOR THE ROSE-GROWER

The rose is probably the most popular of all flowers, and every gardener is sure to find room for one or two trees, bushes, weeping standards, pillars or climbing varieties. Rose-growing is a special study requiring a book to itself. The following notes, however, may assist the general gardener to obtain better results.

Roses like a good soil, so if your soil is light improve it by adding decayed vegetable refuse. If it is heavy, use road grit, wood ashes, old compost, potting soil and mortar.

The site should be prepared in September and in the way suggested for creepers. October is the best planting month, but so long as the weather and soil conditions are suitable planting may be done until, say, March.

Before planting, damaged roots should be cut away and all dead or dying flowers, leaves and buds removed. As in the case of fruit trees, the bottom of the hole opened for the reception of the tree should be slightly rounded upwards, to form a kind of cushion. Bushes should be planted to that depth which allows the junction of the stock and scion to be about 1 in. below the surface ; trees should have their roots only some 2 in. to 4 in. below ground.

Overfeeding is harmful. It should not be necessary to manure newly-planted trees if the site has been properly prepared, but 4 oz. of bone-meal during the winter after planting proves beneficial.

In the autumn a dressing of stable manure or a mixture of basic slag, 4 oz., and kainit, 1½ oz., should be worked into the top soil in the case of established trees.

There are two ways in which rose trees can be fed ; one is by using different artificials at various times throughout the spring and summer, and the other by using a composite chemical fertilizer, at the rate of 3 oz. per square yard in February or March. A suitable preparation consists of super-phosphates, 12 parts ; nitrate of potash, 10 parts ; sulphate of lime, 8 parts ; and sulphate of iron, 1 part.

There are about twenty different kinds of rose and each class or group really requires pruning in a special way. The gardener's best plan is to ask for detailed instructions from the nurseryman when he buys each tree. As a rule, the best time to prune is from the middle of March to the middle of April, and the idea is to cut back weak shoots more severely than strong ones. The cut should always be made in a slanting direction downwards from a bud is facing outwards.

YOUR GARDEN FRIENDS AND FOES

Pests in a garden are of two main kinds, vegetable and animal. Vegetable pests take the form of weeds, and it is the first duty of every gardener to his own garden and his neighbour's to hoe his soil regularly and exterminate weeds as fast as they appear. Long-rooted weeds, such as bindweed, which will not yield to the hoe, must be dug up with a fork and the roots burnt. Daisies, dandelions, and thistles are weeds easy to recognise. Other weeds which might be mistaken by the inexperienced for useful plants are shown in Fig. 4.

INSECTS THAT DESTROY GARDEN PESTS

Animal pests are many and varied and differ widely in appearance and in the plants to which they are harmful. Not all the living creatures a garden contains are pests, however ; some are innocent, while a few are actively helpful in that they destroy the marauders. Centipedes, some beetles, ladybirds, midges, some mites, garden spiders, and earthworms, all perform helpful work and should not be purposely destroyed. Wasps are useful too, unless fruit trees are grown, when they may become a nuisance.

KEEP A HEDGEHOG OR A WATER-TORTOISE

Of the larger animals, a hedgehog and a water-tortoise are particularly active in freeing a garden from insect pests. Both sleep through the winter hidden beneath leaves or a loose pile of refuse. The water tortoise requires a little bath in the summer. The bath, which can be obtained for less than a shilling, should measure 20 in. by 12 and should contain a few loose stones at the side to enable the tortoise to climb in and out. As a rule, there is no need to feed either hedgehog or tortoise since they can get all they require from the garden pests. Neither will touch your plants.

HOMELY REMEDIES FOR COMMON PESTS

There are recognised ways of dealing with almost every pest a garden can produce but not all of them are suitable for a small garden, while some of the preparations required are apt to prove expensive, especially when only small quantities are needed. There are, however, a number of simple remedies which will do much to check garden pests, and every gardener will find others within his means by a little experimenting. The following hints should prove helpful :

1. It is easier to prevent pests than to destroy them when they are in a flourishing state. If you buy good seed and cultivate the soil properly, you go a long way towards checking diseases. When the seedlings appear and the plants begin to grow, keep a careful and frequent eye on them, looking out especially for snails, slugs, and caterpillars. Round holes in a cabbage leaf are sure signs of one or the other. If you pull the leaf upwards and look at its under-side, you will probably see the cause of the trouble clinging there.

All the grubs, slugs, snails, etc., should be picked off by hand as soon as they are seen, and destroyed. Tread them underfoot or, if you are squeamish, put soot or salt on them.

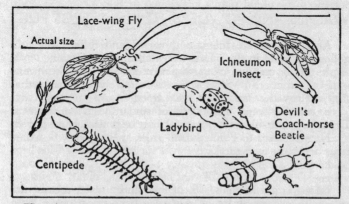

7. *These insects are the gardener's friends and should not be destroyed. They all feed on pests that damage your crops.*

2. Blight, especially the form of it that attacks rose-buds, can be gently rubbed or wiped off when it first appears. Blight is poisonous, so either wear gloves for this job or else be sure you have no cuts or scratches on your fingers when you do it, and disinfect your hands afterwards.

3. The various fly pests are kept under by the use of disinfectants, either in powder or liquid form. Many of these are poisonous and should only be used strictly in accordance with the instructions on the packet. Before having recourse to such strong measures, however, try the effect of salt and water (2 oz. salt to a gallon of water), ordinary soapy water, or any mild household disinfectant.

4. If you are in doubt as to the effect a remedy will have on the infected plants, put the liquid or powder on any stakes or other wood near the plants, instead of on the plants themselves.

5. Disinfectants intended for spraying direct on to the plants can sometimes be used to good effect against ants or similar pests by spraying them underneath stones and on to the soil where the pests live.

6. Boiling water is sometimes effective against woodlice and ants.

7. Some pests can be caught by traps. A jam jar half-filled with water and smeared round the rim with jam or honey will dispose of numbers of wasps. A piece of carrot or turnip fixed in a cleft stick and stuck in the ground will attract wireworms. After a while pull up the stick and burn the bait with its harvest of worms.

WASHES AND POWDERS TO KILL INSECT PESTS

ARSENATE OF LEAD.—Use 1 oz. of powder or paste in 2 gallons of rain-water. Destroys winter moth, lackey moth, apple tortrix, magpie moth, vapourer moth, sawfly grub, and buff-tip moth. *This spray is poisonous and must not be used on fruit and vegetables less than a month before they are gathered.*

BRINE WASH.—A teaspoonful of salt to the gallon of water. Destroys white butterfly grubs of cabbages and other greens.

HELLEBORE OR PYRETHRUM.—Mix 1 oz. with 6 oz. of flour and dust with smoke bellows, such as those used for bees. Make into a solution by mixing 1 oz. in 2 gallons of soapy water. Destroys many different kinds of caterpillar. *Poisonous.*

LIME-SALT.—Make 14 lb. of quicklime into a cream with water, then add $3\frac{1}{2}$ lb. of salt and make up to 10 gallons. Destroys aphides and red spider.

LIME-SULPHUR.—Boil 2 lb. each of lime and flowers of sulphur in a little water for an hour and make up to 10 gallons. Destroys mites, beetles, weevils, and numerous other insect pests.

NICOTINE WASH.—Buy the concentrated solution and dilute as recommended by the salesman. Destroys black fly, green fly, celery fly, sawfly grub, and is an excellent all-round insecticide.

QUASSIA WASH.—Boil 1 lb. of quassia chips in a little water, mix with strong soapy water and dilute to 10 gallons. Used for the same purposes as nicotine wash.

SOAPY WATER.—Take 1 oz. of naphtha or disinfectant soap, boil in a little water and dilute to $\frac{1}{2}$ gallon. Destroys aphides.

WINTER WASHES.—These are caustic washes. (1) Dissolve 1 lb. of caustic soda in 5 gallons of water. (2) Dissolve 1 lb. of caustic soda in 1 gallon of water containing 1 lb. of soft soap and dilute to 8 gallons. These washes destroy aphide eggs, winter and codling moths, weevils, red spider and apple sucker.

MIXTURES TO CURE BLIGHTS AND MILDEWS

BORDEAUX MIXTURE.—Dissolve 1 oz. copper sulphate in a little hot water and pour into 1 gallon of lime-water. Effective against potato blight, leaf curl, leaf spot, mildew and cankers. *Poisonous.*

BURGUNDY MIXTURE.—Dissolve 5 oz. of washing-soda in $\frac{1}{2}$ gallon of warm water ; then dissolve 4 oz. copper sulphate in a little hot water in a wooden vessel, dilute to 2 gallons, and add the first mixture, stirring all the time. Useful as a preventive against the potato disease. *Poisonous.*

LIVER OF SULPHUR.—Dissolve 1 oz. of potassium sulphide in 3 gallons of water. Useful for various fungoid diseases, such as mildew.

SULPHATE OF IRON.—Dissolve 1 oz. in 1 pint of water containing 1 drop of sulphuric acid. Excellent for painting on the wounds left after pruning, for painting on stakes and wooden fences as a preventive against the spread of fungoid diseases, and for application to the soil at the rate of 3 oz. per square yard.

SULPHATE OF COPPER.—Dissolve 1 oz. in 2 gallons of water. A useful fungicide for general use.

WOBURN WASH.—Mix caustic soda, 2 lb ; quicklime, $\frac{1}{4}$ lb. ; sulphate of iron, $\frac{1}{2}$ lb. ; paraffin oil, 5 pints; and water, 10 gallons. Excellent for fruit trees, since it not only cleans the trees of moss and lichens, but also kills many pests.

MIXTURES TO FUMIGATE THE SOIL

Many pests of one kind and another spend some of their time in the soil during the winter, and to eradicate them the soil must be fumigated with suitable materials. Many different substances can be used, but the majority of them can only be applied to vacant land, since they kill or damage the plants as well as the pests.

The one outstanding example of a fumigant which can be used at any time is naphthalene. If this is used " neat," apply $1\frac{1}{2}$ lb. per 30 sq. yds., but it is better to mix 1 lb. with 14 lb. of lime and apply a good handful per square yard. This should be used without fail for a bad pest of wireworms. Two other fumigants which may be used are formalin solution (1 pint to 5 gallons of water) and permanganate of potash (1 oz. to 3 gallons of water).

PESTS THAT ATTACK VEGETABLES

BEAN BEETLES.—These lay eggs on the young pods, the young beetles maturing inside the beans themselves. Picking out the affected beans after the crop has been gathered is all that can be done.

COCKCHAFERS.—The white grub of the cockchafer feeds on many different roots, while the adult eats the foliage. Fumigation of the soil in winter is recommended, but during the summer a dressing of lime and salt in equal parts may be applied.

CABBAGE AND TURNIP FLOWER BEETLES.—These are not of much importance as they consume only the flowers which are not ordinarily required to produce seed. The turnip flea or " hopper " is, however, destructive. The eggs are laid on the first leaves to be grown and the seedlings may be entirely eaten away. Lead arsenate spray is the prescribed treatment.

THE THREE KINDS OF BLIGHT

Three different kinds of blight may be met with—the bean aphis (black fly), cabbage and lettuce aphis, and the powder blight or snowy fly. The first lives on the sap from young flowering shoots, causing a loss of crop ; the second sucks the sap from the heart leaves and the plant usually withers ; the third lives on the sap of many plants, including cabbages and tomatoes. The suggested remedies are early spraying with quassia mixture or tobacco wash and pinching out the growing tips ; dusting with powdered lime and soot ; and spraying with quassia or tobacco wash respectively.

MOTHS AND CATERPILLARS AND THE HARM THEY DO

CABBAGE WHITE BUTTERFLY.—This eats leaves of all greens. Search for the eggs and spray with pyrethrum wash.

CABBAGE MOTH AND YELLOW UNDERWING MOTH.—This devours the leaves of greens at night. Fumigate the soil, spray as for the cabbage white, and pick off by hand.

THE GARDEN SWIFT MOTH.—This moth, or its caterpillars, eats roots, such as potatoes and parsnips. Soil fumigation is the remedy.

THE PEA MOTH.—The grubs of this moth feed on the green pea-pods, entering the soil later as the peas ripen. Burn old peas and stalks.

ROSY RUSTIC MOTH.—Potato haulm or stalk is often almost destroyed by the caterpillars of the rosy rustic moth. Fumigate the soil in winter to destroy the pupæ.

SILVER " Y " MOTH.—Caterpillars of this moth damage beetroots. Pick off the grubs by hand.

THE TURNIP MOTH.—Caterpillars of this moth feed on the leaves and roots of turnips. To destroy, fumigate the soil.

FIVE DISASTROUS MAGGOTS

Five maggots which may prove disastrous are the following :

CABBAGE ROOT FLY.—To eradicate, spray the soil with carbolic and fumigate later.

CARROT FLY.—To prevent, thin the plants early and use deep digging when preparing the site.

CELERY FLY.—To cure, pinch out affected leaves and spray early in the season with tobacco wash to prevent the females laying their eggs.

ONION FLY.—This affects onions and similar plants. Treat as the cabbage root fly.

TURNIP SAWFLY.—Sweep plants lightly with a hand-brush, causing the grubs to fall off, when they will die of starvation.

WEEVILS AND MILLIPEDES

Of the many other pests which attack vegetable crops, the following are those most likely to be encountered :

BEAN AND PEA WEEVILS.—The maggots feed within the flower and young seeds, emerging the following spring as weevils. To prevent, immerse seeds in water before sowing and discard all which float.

EELWORMS.—These feed on the stems of onions and other plants. Burn the affected plants.

MILLIPEDES.—These feed on potatoes, beans and carrots. To eradicate, fumigate the soil during the summer months.

TURNIP GALL WEEVILS.—These affect cabbages as well as turnips. The cure is to burn old stumps and " galled " roots.

FRUIT-LOVING INSECTS

A VERY large number of insect pests attack the various kinds of fruit, doing a great deal of damage. The following is a list of the most usual, with suggestions for preventing their appearance or destroying them after they have arrived :

FRUIT BEETLES AND WEEVILS

APPLE BLOSSOM WEEVIL.—This feeds in the heart of the buds. Burn withered flowers and use a lime wash.

RASPBERRY BEETLE.—This causes the fruits to fall. Gather the dropped fruits and burn.

RASPBERRY WEEVIL.—This pest feeds at the root of many different plants, while the adults live on young shoots and flowers. Catch the beetles after dusk and kill by dropping them in paraffin oil.

BLIGHTS WHICH ATTACK LEAVES AND BRANCHES

Blights include the currant and gooseberry aphides which result in the leaves withering and the fruit dropping off. Apply paraffin emulsion before the leaves begin to curl up.

The fruit tree aphides are sap-feeders on stem, leaf and fruit. Spray in early summer and apply a carbolic wash in winter.

On soft-barked apples a trouble which may be encountered is the woolly aphis which produces canker-galls on the root and branch. Paint the patches with methylated spirits and use a lime-sulphur wash.

DESTRUCTIVE CATERPILLARS AND THEIR TREATMENT

The most important and most destructive of the caterpillars are the March moth, mottled moth, November moth and winter moth, for these are all leaf-eaters and flower-eaters during the early summer months. To control, spray with lead arsenate in the spring, and fumigate the soil.

Other troublesome moths are the codling moth, of which the grubs feeds within the fruit in summer ; the currant moth, gooseberry moth, lackey moth, magpie moth and raspberry moth. Soil fumigation in winter, picking off affected shoots and burning, and the application of an arsenate spray is the treatment for all of them.

MAGGOTS AND MITES

There are numerous maggots, including the apple sawfly, pear and cherry sawfly, pear midge and plum fruit moth, but if the soil is fumigated in winter these should not prove troublesome.

Of the mites, the three following are the most usual :

CURRANT GALL MOTH.—Spray with liver of sulphur and burn the infected bushes.

PEAR LEAF BLISTER MITE.—Use a combined lime-sulphur and caustic winter wash.

RED SPIDER.—Use a nicotine wash in summer and caustic spray in winter.

The brown scale insect which feeds on the sap of currants and the mussel scale which sucks sap from the bark of trees are both controlled by using a paraffin wash in summer and a caustic spray in winter.

ENEMIES IN THE FLOWER-BEDS

THERE is a very large number of insects which prey on flowers of various kinds. The names of the principal ones are given below but in general it is not necessary to know insects by name to tell when they are doing harm. The use of naphthalene[1] to fumigate the soil will do a great deal to prevent the majority of pests, since many of them live in the soil during the winter months. Once the pests make their appearance, treatment is along the lines indicated at the beginning of this section and should be applied without delay.

PESTS THAT DESTROY YOUR FLOWERS

BEETLES.—Rose beetle, garden chafer, red-legged weevil.

BLIGHTS.—Aphides and leaf-hoppers, the cuckoo-spit insect and thrips.

CATERPILLARS.—Bell moth, buff ermine moth, buff-tip moth, garden carpet moth, green-veined butterfly, large and small angle-shade moth, little ermine moth, pug moth, spectacle moth, swallowtail moth, tortrix moth, waved umber moth, white ermine moth and vapourer moth.

MAGGOTS.—Brown grub, carnation fly, chrysanthemum fly, green rose maggot, laburnum miner, narcissus fly, red rose maggot, St. Mark's fly and yellow grub.

[1] See page 77.

YOUR JOB MONTH BY MONTH

THERE are numerous jobs which call for attention throughout the year, such as collecting refuse for burning or making into compost, and general tidying up. These tasks will be done when there is a minute to spare and as they become urgent. There are many others, however, which must be done at the right time if they are to be of any use while some jobs, essential to successful gardening, may easily be overlooked unless a programme is mapped out and consulted regularly. The following time-table gives the principal jobs that have to be done each month :

JANUARY.—Make up all arrears of digging, particularly if animal manure or a manure substitute is being incorporated in the soil.

Apply insecticides and fungicides and fumigate the soil now and at intervals throughout the year as required. Give a dressing of lime this month or next.

The major work in connection with the fruit trees is pruning the red and white currant bushes, if this was not done in December.

Among the flowers the main task is to strike perpetual flowering carnation cuttings under glass.

FEBRUARY.—If the district is a mild and well-protected one, make a sowing of summer cauliflowers, leeks and carrots. Sow early peas and celery under glass, and plant shallots.

Make trenches for peas, runner beans, and celery.

The first weeds will be making their appearance, so start hoeing, continuing as called for in the months following.

Cut out unwanted branches from the gooseberry bushes.

MARCH.—Sowing begins in earnest this month. Here is a list of the seeds to put in : Summer cabbages, carrots, autumn cauliflowers, early peas and main-crop peas, onions, parsnips, turnips (catch-crop), carrots (catch-crop), salad onions, saladings, summer spinach (catch-crop), annual and biennial herbs.

The early and main-crop potatoes should be planted.

Prune newly-planted apple trees and apply chemical manure to established apples and pears. Prune blackberries, loganberries and raspberries. Prune young currant bushes.

Roses should be pruned this month and the first hardy annuals sown.

APRIL.—If some of the seeds on the March list could not be planted in time, make up arrears now. Sow also summer cabbages, early savoys, brussels sprouts, broccoli, kale, main-crop peas (for succession), celery, carrots, beets, saladings and summer spinach (for succession).

Plant out March-sown summer cabbages.

Plant out home-raised or bought summer cauliflowers.

Plant main-crop potatoes early in the month.

Sow hardy annuals, including sweet peas.

Finish striking indoor chrysanthemum cuttings, a task which should have been carried out regularly since November.

Prune roses.

MAY.—Sow late savoys, main-crop peas (for succession), runner and French beans, leeks, beets, saladings, summer spinach (for succession).

Plant out April sown summer cabbages, brussels sprouts, and autumn cauliflowers.

JUNE.—To maintain a regular supply, make further sowings of runner and French beans, summer spinach and saladings.

Plant out early savoys, late savoys, broccoli, kale.

Make a start earthing-up the early potatoes.

If tomatoes are to be grown in the open buy the necessary plants and plant out.

JULY.—Sow saladings. Sow spring cabbages (follow-on crop).

Harvest shallots.

Ripen and harvest onions.

Cut out old raspberry canes ; prune red and white currant bushes.

AUGUST.—Make the last sowing of the saladings.

Sow winter lettuce and onions (follow-on crops).

Prune established apple, pear, and plum trees.

Mulch blackberries and loganberries.

Sow annuals and biennials.

Increase outdoor chrysanthemums by cuttings.

Plant bulbs in fibre.

SEPTEMBER.—There is nothing of importance to be done among the vegetables during this month except apply the hoe, water as necessary, and harvest any crops which are ready.

Prune established blackberries and loganberries.

Cut out old wood of black currants.

Plant in fibre any bulbs which were not obtainable last month.

Prepare sites for creepers and rose trees.

OCTOBER.—Two vegetable sowings should be made this month—prickly spinach and broad beans—as follow-on crops.

Plant out spring cabbages and winter lettuce.

Start collecting leaves for making into leaf-mould.

Earth-up the celery.

Plant fruit trees.

Lift and root-prune fruit trees planted the season before.

Apply liquid manure to cherry trees.

Mulch fruit trees.

Increase perennials by root division.

Remove perpetual border carnations to greenhouse and pot-up.

Increase outdoor chrysanthemums by root division.

Plant creepers and rose trees.

NOVEMBER.—This is the time when the annual digging should be started—and completed, if possible.

Continue collecting leaves.

Plant fruit trees and bushes.

Apply liquid manure to established apple and pear trees ; artificial manures if the natural variety is unobtainable.

Prepare trenches for sweet peas.

Begin striking indoor chrysanthemum cuttings.

DECEMBER.—Sprout second-early potatoes.

Continue digging.

Prune established apple and pear trees and partly-grown cherry trees.

Prune red and white currants.

POULTRY-KEEPING IN WAR-TIME

SINCE the beginning of the war commercial poultry-keepers and others working on a large scale, such as specialist breeders, have experienced great difficulties. It is a regrettable fact that the poultry stock of the country was considerably reduced during the six months immediately following the outbreak of hostilities.

The principal reason for this is that food supplies have been short but, since the greater proportion of the foods commonly used are imported, a decrease in supplies was only to be expected.

Despite these facts—really because of them—the war-time home food-producer is strongly urged to keep a good flock of layers on the allotment plot or in the garden. The price of new-laid eggs has, of course, been higher since the war started than under normal conditions and, in spite of feeding difficulties, the allotment-holder or home gardener can actually produce eggs at a cost considerably below that charged in the shops. These eggs cannot be sold without a licence but, since eggs are such a valuable item of food, a sufficient number of fowls should be maintained to provide the household with all it requires, with a surplus during the most productive seasons which can be preserved for a season of scarcity.

OVERCOMING WAR-TIME FEEDING PROBLEMS

The food scarcity need not trouble the small poultry-keeper unduly because fowls have a wonderful way of converting various kinds of waste material into first-class eggs. More than half of the food necessary to keep layers in health and heavy production can consist of house scraps and vegetables, while substitutes for the meals normally used are still available in sufficient quantity.

Those who have read in their newspapers, therefore, that the poultry-keeping industry is almost on its last legs and consequently felt discouraged from trying to provide birds and eggs for their own tables, may take heart again. There are many ways of overcoming the food problem so that the allotment or garden flock of laying-birds will produce plenty of eggs at pre-war cost, and keep the family supplied all the year round.

TO HOUSE THE LAYING BIRDS

FORMERLY the usual method of keeping chickens on a small scale was to provide them with a house and run or, where space permitted, to allow them to wander in yard or field. There are several different methods in use to-day, varying according to the purpose for which the birds are kept and the space available. Obviously the owner of a small garden or allotment cannot allow the birds the freedom of his crops and, where space is limited and egg production the main object, the intensive method—that is the keeping of the birds in a single house, allowing so much space to each, and without a run—is the one recommended. It would not, of course, be suitable for breeding poultry, which is one reason why the owner of the small garden or allotment is advised not to attempt breeding.

The size of house must naturally depend upon the number of fowls to be kept, but more space in proportion is required for a few fowls than for many. For a small flock of layers, say, ten to a dozen, each bird must be allowed about $5\frac{1}{2}$ sq. ft. of floor space when the average height to the roof is 6 ft. A house for a dozen fowls, therefore, need not be larger than 8 ft. long by 8 ft. deep. If a larger number of fowls is kept the length of the shed should be increased, but not its depth ; that is, from back to front. It is suggested that, if convenient, the poultry house should be placed in the north-east corner of the plot, as shown in Fig. 1.

The best type of house for the intensive culture recommended is that shown in Fig. 8. This is a lean-to structure and takes the form of a roosting house and scratching-shed combined. Assuming that a dozen fowls are to be kept, the dimensions will be 8 ft. from back to front, 8 ft. long (more, if necessary), $5\frac{1}{2}$ ft. high at the back and $6\frac{1}{2}$ ft. high in the front. The back, two ends and lower part of the front should be solid. Two-thirds of the front should, however, be filled in with wire-netting, one-half—the lower half—of the netted opening being covered by two glazed windows which, hinged at the bottom, can be opened in fine weather. The upper part of the netted area is protected by the drip-shutter shown in the picture, and this should protrude at an angle of about 45 degrees, allowing all moisture to run away easily.

LETTING IN AIR AND KEEPING OUT DRAUGHTS

One of the most difficult things to arrange with the gable poultry house is efficient ventilation, because sufficient fresh

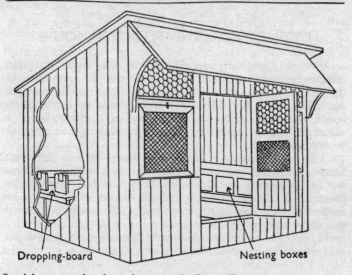

Dropping-board   Nesting boxes

8. *A lean-to poultry house is automatically ventilated, for stale air rises, follows the slope of the roof, and escapes through the wire netting in front. Part of the left-hand wall has been opened to show the position of the perches and the droppings-board below.*

air must be allowed to enter, but there must be no trace of a draught. The lean-to house is recommended, because it is automatically ventilated. The perches are placed at the back. When the birds are roosting the exhaled breath, being warm, rises to the roof, follows the upward slope and passes out through the netted front. The flow of air is dependent upon the number of birds in the shed. In any case, every inmate is assured of obtaining plenty of fresh air — without a draught.

The poultry house should be built of stout material. Use 1-in. thick boarding for the walls and roof, and cover the roof with a first-quality roofing felt. The outside of the poultry house should be treated with some reliable wood preservative, such as one of the special tar preparations sold for this purpose. Paint looks well, but is rather expensive. A wooden floor is a necessity, because as the birds are kept intensively the only way in which they can secure the necessary exercise is by scratching for the grain part of their ration, which should be buried under a goodly depth of straw or other suitable litter. The boarding for the floor should be at least 1 in. thick, but it is better if rather thicker.

FITTINGS FOR THE POULTRY HOUSE

Perches must be provided, but as the layers are kept intensively and the cost of the house must be kept down to the minimum the whole of the floor space should be free as a scratching area. For this reason there should be a droppings-board some 5 in. below the roosts. If the droppings-board is raised about 20 in. above the floor the birds can get underneath without difficulty.

The best perches are those constructed of 2 in. by 2 in. battens with the two top corners rounded off so as to give the birds a fair grip-hold. The droppings-board should be constructed of $\frac{3}{4}$-in. material and the whole fitting should be made so that it can be removed easily. The droppings-board should be kept covered with a liberal sprinkling of sand or dry earth, for this makes the removal of the excreta easier—a job that should be attended to every second day or so.

TO CHOOSE AND FURNISH NEST-BOXES

Nest-boxes must also be provided. There should be one nest for every three or four layers. The boxes are usually built in series. They should be 1 ft. square, 12 in. high in front and 15 in. high at the back. It is better to make them floorless, standing them on a shelf 18 in. above the floor level and about 18 in. wide so that the birds are provided with an alighting-board in front. This makes it easier for them to reach the nests and minimises the risk of their breaking any eggs which may have been laid before their entry.

The nest-boxes must be furnished with some sort of litter. Short straw, broken in the hands, is generally used (hay is unsuitable as it forms too good a harbourage for insect pests) but straw-mats are preferable. These mats are more or less like split straw wine-bottle covers, consisting of straw woven with string. They are inexpensive yet possess numerous advantages over loose straw. The latter is often scratched out by the hens when settling themselves down for the business of laying and, if the wooden floor of the nest is bare, eggs may get broken. The loose straw has to be renewed at fairly frequent intervals ; straw mats are very durable, and if one should get slightly soiled or fouled it can be washed in disinfectant water and dried and used again.

THE BEST KINDS OF FEEDING UTENSILS

Other fitments include wet mash troughs (dry mash feeding is not a practical proposition for the war-time home food-producer), water vessels and boxes for shell, grit and granulated vegetable charcoal. Wet mash troughs should be V-shaped with each side 6 in. wide, and stout wood of 1 in. thickness should be employed. The end pieces should be made square and of fair size, say, 10 in. long, so as to prevent the birds tipping the troughs over. Provide sufficient troughs to allow each bird 10 in. of space—when wet mash is fed all the birds eat at the same time, hence the need for large troughs.

Various kinds of water vessel can be obtained. In the case of a small intensive house, such as the allotment-holder is likely to use, those types which hang on the wall are preferable to those which stand on the floor. If non-hanging water-containers are used they should be stood on legged platforms, so that none of the floor space is occupied. Layers consume a considerable quantity of water—eggs consist of about 90 per cent water—but if it is very cold they drink sufficient only for their body needs, and egg production is adversely affected. It is advisable, therefore, to have a small heater (excellent ones can be bought at a very reasonable price) for each water vessel so that the temperature may be maintained about 10 degrees above freezing point, even in the coldest weather.

Small boxes for the oyster-shell, grit and charcoal can be attached to the walls. A series of three boxes, each one measuring 6 in. long by 4 in. wide and 3 in. deep, will probably be found most convenient, but individual ones of the same size may be used if preferred.

Oyster-shell or cockle-shell are both good ; limestone grit is better than granite or flint grit ; and the granulated vegetable charcoal should be graded to about the size of a pea.

THE PURPOSE OF THE DUST-BATH

One further fitment is necessary. This is a dust-bath. Birds in their wild state keep their bodies free of insect pests by dusting themselves in dry earth ; intensively kept birds cannot do this. A dust-bath is simply a box filled with a mixture of sand, dry earth, road grit or similar materials, together with a liberal dusting of insect powder. The most convenient place is usually a corner of the house—raised above the floor level some 18 in. A suitable size is for the two sides adjacent to the walls to be 3 ft. in length with the third side rather more than 4 ft. The box should be 10 in. deep and be filled with about 5 in. of dusting material.

HOW TO CHOOSE YOUR BIRDS

THERE are dozens of different breeds of domesticated fowls and well over a hundred different varieties, but there is no need to mention the majority of them, since they are not suitable for the object which the allotment-holder or garden poultry-keeper has in mind—the production of eggs.

Apart from the purely fancy or exhibition breeds and the table varieties (specially bred for years with the main object of increasing the quantity and quality of flesh and always at the expense of the number of eggs laid) the utility breeds can be divided into two classes—the heavy breeds and the light breeds of which the latter may be preferred.

THE PROS AND CONS OF " HEAVIES " AND " LIGHTS "

The heavy breeds, such as the Wyandotte, Rhode Island Red, Plymouth Rock, Buff Rock, Light Sussex and Orpington, lay tinted or brown-shelled eggs, and a considerable proportion of their eggs are produced during the winter months when egg prices are high. They also become broody ; that is, they want to sit and hatch out a brood of chickens in the spring. To a certain extent this is a disadvantage, because a broody hen does not lay, but it is not a difficult matter to break a broody hen if she is taken in hand in time.

The light breeds, such as the Leghorn and Ancona, lay white-shelled eggs ; they are not usually such good winter layers—but (as a general rule) they do not go broody. They are smaller birds and the culled pullets are not as good for eating as those belonging to the heavy breeds.

A BREED TO MEET ALL HOUSEHOLD NEEDS

Plenty of eggs throughout the year, with a goodly number during the winter, a few boiling fowls in late summer and early autumn and an occasional roasting fowl, sums up the requirements of the average family. Light breed birds, as mentioned, do not carry a great amount of flesh, nor are they particularly good winter layers. The choice should, therefore, be in the direction of one of the heavy breeds. The old hens are excellent, for they are of the cut-and-come-again variety, and should there be a pullet which is not up to standard and is culled it makes a capital roaster.

As to which breed is decided upon there is little to be said, because there is not much to choose between the different ones named. The order of preference might be as follows : White Wyandotte, Rhode Island Red, Light Sussex, Buff Rock, Barred or Plymouth Rock and Buff Orpington.

FAMILY CHARACTERISTICS OF FIRST IMPORTANCE

What is really of greater importance than actual breed is the strain or family. There are numerous strains which have been scientifically bred for years, and heavy laying and other good characteristics have not only been passed on from one generation to another, but improved.

When making a start with poultry the birds should be bought from a reputable breeder and they should be of the highest quality the pocket can afford. Half-grown pullets of really grand stock can be purchased in the summer for 5s. to 6s. each ; about-to-lay pullets in September cost about twice as much.

The prospective poultry-keeper is warned strongly against buying pullets or any other fowls in the local market. Such birds are practically always the " throw-outs " of some breeder's yard and so almost worthless, while it is impossible to determine whether they have a clean bill of health or not. It is a sheer waste of money to buy inferior stock of this description. The war-time poultry-keeper is advised *not* to buy day-old chickens and rear them to maturity, but if he does the same advice holds good—never buy such chickens in the local market even if the price is only 3s. or 4s. a dozen.

If the garden or allotment is situated in a town it is better to choose a dark-coloured breed, such as the Rhode Island Red or Barred Rock, since light-plumaged fowls always look dowdy when kept in smoky surroundings.

When buying stock make a point of ordering some time in advance so that the pick of the breeder's pullets is obtained (according to the price paid, of course) ; delay may mean that not-quite-so-good fowls remain, and although a somewhat lower price may be charged for them they cannot prove so satisfactory in the end.

WHEN BIRDS BEGIN TO LAY

Bred-to-lay pullets of the heavy breeds which are hatched out towards the end of February and during the first two weeks of March start laying about the beginning of the following October and continue until July or August, when they fall into their first moult. Until this stage is reached they are called pullets. Hens is the word used to denote pullets which have moulted and entered on their second season of laying.

Pullets are better layers than hens. The profitable laying life of a fowl is two seasons ; that is, until it is from twenty-eight to thirty months old. It is not an economic practice, however, to discard the pullets at the end of their first laying season ; neither is it economic for the whole flock to consist of second-season stock.

It is suggested that the original flock consist of one-half pullets and one-half hens, or thereabouts, because it may be found that one or two of the pullets fail to " make the pace " and have to be discarded before they are through their first laying season. Pullets and hens should be housed separately, when possible, but can be kept together when necessary.

ENSURING A STEADY SUPPLY OF EGGS

The best plan to adopt is to purchase half-grown pullets in the summer to the extent of one-half the number of birds to be kept, and a month or two later to buy second-season hens which, by the way, cost less than pullets. The following year the hens can be killed and eaten (this should happen before they fall into their second moult, say, from July to September) and at the same time half-grown pullets should be purchased to take their place. The great advantage of following this plan is that production throughout the year is more consistent and periods of scarcity need not occur.

WHY THE SMALLHOLDER SHOULD NOT BREED LAYERS

It will be noticed that mention has been made only of buying half-grown or mature stock. The reason is that it is a mistake for the war-time gardening poultry-keeper to attempt to breed his own layers by buying or producing hatching eggs.

The allotment flock of layers is kept intensively and birds kept under such conditions, no matter how good they are as layers, do not make satisfactory breeders. To buy hatching eggs—and the same is true of buying day-old chicks—involves a considerable outlay for appliances, while it is impossible to find the necessary room for rearing the youngsters as they should be reared. A further point in connection with producing hatching eggs at home is that the only cock worth having costs anything from £3 to £5. Strain of the cock is even more important than that of the hens as regards its effect on the laying capacity of the progeny, so that it is useless to attempt to breed layers from an inferior bird.

HOW TO FEED THE LAYING BIRDS

IT would serve no good purpose to give particulars regarding the way in which layers were fed in pre-war days, because a number of the foods are not obtainable, while others are so high in price as to prohibit their use.

The only suggestions made here are for feeding the layers under prevailing conditions so that they will give a good account of themselves, lay a large number of eggs and, at the same time, keep healthy.

The two most important considerations are that the food provided must be palatable (laying fowls consume a large quantity of food every day, usually in the neighbourhood of 5 oz.) and it must provide all the necessary nutritive elements in the right proportions.

FOUR KINDS OF FOOD THAT ARE ESSENTIAL

Foods are divided into four groups—flesh-forming ; heat-producing and energy-creating ; bulking foods ; and what are generally termed basic foods (foods which are more or less well balanced). An excess of any one group is disastrous.

It is essential to know what kinds of food belong to each group because, although certain sample mashes are suggested, the poultry-keeper must make use of those foods which happen to be available in the district, and if he cannot obtain one or two kinds in a group he may substitute others in that group. What he must *not* do is to substitute foods in one group for foods in another.

The flesh-forming foods consist of both animal and vegetable products—some of each should be used. The ones obtainable under war-time conditions are : Fish meal, meat meal, whale meal, dried blood, dried milk products (dried skim milk, dried buttermilk and dried whey), and possibly meat scraps from the house, although meat is rationed. The vegetable foods belonging to this class are soya bean meal, pea and bean meals, dried yeast, palm kernel meal, linseed cake meal, coconut cake meal and husked earth-nut meal.

The heat-producing and energy-creating meals are maize meal, maize germ meal, maize gluten meal, ground oats, barley meal, rice meal, potato meal, cooked potatoes, rye meal and tapioca meal.

The usual bulking foods (these also provide mineral salts) are bran, clover meal, alfalfa meal, root vegetables, green vegetables, malt culms and brewers' grains.

The basic foods are middlings (called sharps, thirds, pollard, toppings, etc., in different parts of the country), wheat meal, sugar beet pulp, biscuit meal, rye middlings and dari meal.

KEEPING THE DIET BALANCED

When using any of the foods named the poultry-keeper should use them in definite proportions. Without being too exact, the plan should be to make the mash of 1 part by weight of flesh-formers, 3 parts of heat-producers, 4 parts of basic food and 2 parts of bulking food.

The allotment or garden plot will provide a considerable quantity of refuse or waste food for the fowls. Table and kitchen scraps may also be used successfully. The first will consist of potatoes, carrots and greens for the most part; the second of scraps of bread, scones, cakes, porridge, puddings, meat trimmings and fish waste.

SOME SAMPLE MASHES

Here are a few sample mashes which will suggest how use can be made of a variety of different materials.

Potatoes should be the great standby, because if sufficient are not grown in the garden or allotment it is usually possible to buy " chat " or small potatoes at a nominal price. This is an excellent formula : Potatoes (weighed before cooking), 4 parts by weight ; carrots (or swedes if they can be bought cheaply), 2 parts ; palm kernel meal, pea or bean meal, $\frac{1}{2}$ part ; fish meal, meat meal or dried blood, $\frac{1}{2}$ part. The meal or dried blood should be cooked in as little water as possible, and then dried off with equal parts of barley meal, middlings and bran (if bran is not obtainable sugar beet pulp can be used). Extra barley meal may be used if middlings are difficult to buy.

Since potatoes are likely to be comparatively plentiful, another mash containing them may be given : Potatoes, 3 parts by weight ; shredded cabbage or kale, 1 part ; dried brewer's grains, 1 part ; ground oats, barley meal or wheat meal, 1 part ; and one of the animal flesh-formers, $\frac{1}{2}$ part.

Those who live in a country district may be able to buy fairly coarse ground oats, barley and peas or beans from a local farmer. In such a case the following mash is recommended : Ground oats, 3 parts by weight ; ground barley, 2 parts ; pea or bean meal, 1 part ; and one of the animal flesh-formers, $\frac{1}{2}$ part.

If there are plenty of roots and cabbages and other greens as well as ample supplies of house scraps, the mash might well consist of carrots or other roots, cabbage or other greens, 2 parts ; house scraps, 4 parts ; potato peelings, 1 part ; and an animal flesh-former, 1 part, the whole being dried off with middlings or barley meal.

Fish meal, meat meal and other animal flesh-formers are getting more expensive every day, so it may be necessary in some instances to dispense with them altogether. In this case a satisfactory mash can be made of bran or sugar beet pulp,

1 part by weight ; malt culms or brewers' grains, 1 part ; wheat meal and ground oats, each 1½ parts ; potatoes, 3 parts ; barley meal, 1 part ; soya bean meal, ½ part ; and earth-nut meal, ½ part.

It is difficult to say much regarding the grains which should be used, since wheat, for one, is banned nowadays. Of the others, barley, oats, dari and kibbled maize (the price of this is likely to rise still higher as the war proceeds) may be used. The poultry-keeper should purchase a good sample of the most reasonably priced grain obtainable in his district.

Green food—fresh, tender, crisp garden produce—should be fed every day unless this is incorporated in the mash. Green food is not only a first-class food, but it is also a tonic and provides necessary minerals.

HOW TO GIVE THE FOOD

Intensively kept layers should be encouraged to take a lot of exercise, so it is advisable to feed grain first thing in the morning, burying this underneath the floor litter, so that the birds are kept busy for some hours. The morning allowance of grain should be 1¾ oz. for each bird or, if a midday feed of ½ oz. is given, allow 1¼ oz. first thing in the morning. About noon green food should be supplied—say, about ¾ oz. per bird per day.

Mash should be fed in the late afternoon and it should be of the consistency known as crumbly-moist (it can be formed into a ball in the hand, but the ball breaks to pieces when thrown into the trough) and the layers should be allowed to eat as they will. In winter, if a midday meal of grain is not provided, a small feed of wet mash should be given—2½ oz. per bird of the prepared mash is correct. In summer the late afternoon feed of wet mash may well be followed by a small meal (½ oz.) of grain, supplied in troughs.

KEEPING YOUR BIRDS IN GOOD CONDITION

Certain special precautions and care in the general management of the birds will well repay the poultry-keeper. The interior of the layers' house should be whitewashed three or four times a year, the wash containing a liberal addition of disinfectant. Spraying paraffin, from time to time, in possible lurking places of mites is also recommended.

Cleaning is an essential duty. The droppings-board should be scraped clean every second or third day and a little fresh soil or sand put down. The food and water utensils should be washed out daily and scalded out once a week.

An important factor in the health of the birds (and therefore in their rate of production) is freedom from body parasites. The two principal parasites which attack the fowls are lice and mites. The former live all the time on their hosts ; the latter spend the daylight hours in crevices in the woodwork and in the perch sockets, coming out at night to prey upon the birds. Mites are blood-suckers and quickly lower vitality, reducing the condition of any bird on which they feed.

The provision of a dust-bath goes a long way towards enabling the birds to keep themselves reasonably free of lice, but this naturally does not affect the mites, since at the time the birds take their baths they are in their breeding quarters.

TWO WAYS OF DESTROYING PARASITES

It is possible, however, to kill off both lice and mites at one time. There are two ways of doing this. An hour after the birds have gone to roost they should be individually dusted with sodium flouride. A little pinch should be rubbed into the fluff at the base of the tail, round the vent, under the wings and at the base of the neck.

The second plan is to paint a narrow streak down the centre of each perch with a nicotine sulphate preparation. If this is done half an hour or so before the birds go to roost the heat of their bodies causes fumes to rise and these kill off both lice and mites. The sodium flouride or the nicotine paint should be used twice at an interval of a week or ten days.

The crevices in the woodwork should also be sprayed with paraffin oil on two or three occasions at weekly intervals to destroy the mites' breeding places.

The best floor litter is straw, but this is rather expensive, so whenever dried leaves or bracken are obtainable they should be used. The litter should be put down to a depth of about 6 in., and it must be renewed as soon as it begins to " mat " owing to its excessive content of manure. The litter should be forked over daily so as to aerate and dry it.

DRYING AND STORING FOWL MANURE

Every scrap of manure produced by the fowls must be stored and, later on, used on the vegetable plots. As previously mentioned, the droppings are in two forms—mixed with a little earth or sand from under the perches, and mixed with the floor litter. The former is best used as a top-dressing ; the latter for incorporating with the soil at the time of the annual autumn or winter digging.

The " neat " manure should be air-dried by being placed in shallow wooden trays ; when dry it can be stored in sacks. The littery manure may either be kept by itself or added to the compost heap, or the leaf-mould heap if the litter consists of leaves or bracken.

"BREAKING" THE BROODY HEN

The poultry-keeper who is keeping birds intensively will not want to do any hatching or rearing, so every hen which evinces a desire to sit should be broken of her habit as quickly as possible. If treated at once a broody should start laying again in four or five days; if left for a week or more it may be a month before she begins.

Place the hen in a box, say, 18 in. square by 21 in. high, made with a sparred front and a sparred bottom (the spars should not be wider than 1 in.), and fitted with a small food trough and a water vessel. Hang the box on the wall of the house—inside during the winter and spring, but outside in the summer—so that the incipient broody hen can see her mates enjoying themselves scratching.

Feed the hen in the usual way so that she is in fit condition to produce eggs when she gives up her wish to sit.

GETTING THE MOULTING SEASON OVER QUICKLY

Casting the old feathers and growing a new lot is a perfectly natural process and, provided the fowls are managed properly and fed correctly, few experience any difficulty in making the change in a matter of six weeks or thereabouts. Some of the layers, chiefly the older birds, may start moulting a little earlier than the others. When pullets and hens are kept in the same house, however, it is a nuisance when they moult at different times. It is suggested, therefore, that when it is noticed that a few feathers are lying about all the birds should be encouraged to moult together. This can be done by reducing the quantity of wet mash supplied or cutting it out entirely for a week or ten days. This usually causes the birds to cease laying and then they moult.

It is worth adding 5 per cent. of linseed meal to the mash when the feathers are falling freely, continuing with this until the birds are fully reclothed. A tonic may be given, and one which proves useful at this time consists of cascarilla bark, 2 oz.; aniseed, $\frac{1}{2}$ oz.; pimento, 1 oz.; malt dust, 2 oz.; and carbonate of iron, 1 oz. The above ingredients should be mixed with four times their bulk of sugar and a sprinkling added to the mash every day for a couple of weeks.

Rake over the floor litter two or three times a day and collect and burn all cast feathers. These may have a few lice on them and unless removed may infest the fowls afterwards.

TO KILL AND PREPARE A BIRD FOR TABLE

A chicken can be killed either by striking it sharply and heavily on the head with a stout stick or similar instrument, or by cutting its throat. The latter method is used to procure whiter meat but, if it is adopted, the bird should first be stunned by a blow on the head.

As soon as the chicken has been killed it should be hung up by the legs with the head hanging downwards to allow the blood to run out. Outside the back door, out of reach of a cat, is a suitable place. When most of the blood has run out, and while the chicken is still warm, it should be plucked. Hold the fowl with the head towards you, and the legs away from you, and pull out the feathers towards the head. The feathers can be removed quite easily with the exception, perhaps, of those on the wings, which may give a little more trouble.

Next cut off the head and draw out the intestines, making sure you leave nothing behind or the bird will have a bitter flavour when cooked. The liver, heart and gizzard can be kept for making gravy or using in some other dish, and any eggs, of course, may be used ; the rest of the insides are unfit for human consumption. Cut off the feet of the bird.

Finally go over it with a lighted taper, singeing slightly to remove the hairs. Pull any obstinate quills with tweezers. The bird is then ready for trussing and cooking.

TO TREAT POULTRY AILMENTS

IF one of the birds is seen to be off-colour pick it up and keep it by itself until the complaint from which it is suffering can be diagnosed—it may be nothing, but it may be serious.

Any bird suffering from a really serious trouble should be killed at once, because to attempt a cure may not prove successful, while in any case it is sure to be a lengthy business and during the whole time of illness and convalescence the layer is out of production and so not profit-earning.

When the half-grown pullets or any other birds are bought keep them by themselves for ten days, no matter how much trouble this involves. Imported birds are always liable to introduce some complaint or disease ; discover whether they have a clean bill of health by isolating them before adding them to the laying flock.

Domesticated poultry are subject to many and varied ailments and diseases, but provided cleanliness is maintained and the birds are managed and fed properly, no serious epidemic should break out. The following treatments for everyday ailments likely to be encountered will prevent many losses if applied promptly.

BRONCHITIS.—This complaint is due to exposure to dampness and often begins with a slight cold ; the symptoms are rapid breathing, rattling in the throat and a cough. Give two grains of black antimony daily in the mash and place a jug of boiling water close to the box or cage in which the patient is kept.

BUMBLE FOOT.—A condition caused by an inadequate supply of suitable litter on the floor or infection through a cut. The symptoms are lameness and an abscess on the ball of the foot. Open abscess, squeeze out the pus, wash with bichloride of mercury and bandage.

COLDS.—These are due to dampness of litter or bad ventilation. The symptoms are running at the eyes and nostrils and sneezing. Wash affected parts with a 3 per cent. solution of boracic acid and inject eucalyptus oil.

CONSTIPATION.—This ailment is caused by lack of exercise and green food. The vent is plugged with hard excreta. Give 25 grains of Epsom salts.

DIARRHŒA.—A symptom of numerous complaints, serious and otherwise. Add a little powdered chalk to the mash after giving a mild purgative.

INDIGESTION.—Improper or over-feeding causes this complaint. The only symptom is that the bird appears to be dumpish and lazy. Correct the rations and make up a mixture of pulverised gentian, $\frac{1}{2}$ lb ; ginger, 2 oz. ; saltpetre, 2 oz. ; and iron sulphate, 4 oz. Give a tablespoonful to every 3 quarts of mash.

SCALY LEG.—This is caused by a mite living under the scales of the leg. The legs become encrusted with rough, whitish, enlarged scale areas. Dip affected parts in a mixture of equal parts of paraffin oil and raw linseed oil, but take care not to allow the liquid to touch the flesh above the hock.

PRESERVING THE SURPLUS EGG SUPPLY

As only one flock of layers is kept there may be a slight scarcity of eggs when the birds are moulting, while if the winter is very severe the birds may not lay so heavily as expected. But as against this probably more eggs are produced in the spring than can be consumed in the house.

The solution of this somewhat inconsistent supply problem is, however, a simple one. Surplus eggs in the spring should be preserved so that they are available as required at any time during the next six months or so.

Preserving eggs is a simple business, while the slight cost is fully justified, since it means a continuous supply of first-class eggs. If the following hints are adopted, all chance of failure will be ruled out.

Practically any kind of utensil may be used, but the special metal buckets, fitted with wire baskets, made for the purpose, are preferable to anything else. Wooden pails, large crocks and the like may be used if obtainable at a low price.

A CHEAP AND SIMPLE METHOD

The most suitable of the many preservatives for the war-time poultry-keeper is waterglass. This is not expensive, and quite small tins can be purchased. It is desirable, however, to have a preserving fluid of the correct strength. After long experience, the writer suggests that ¾ lb. should be dissolved in a gallon of hot water, this being allowed to cool before being used, although the usual strength recommended is 1 lb. per gallon.

The eggs must be absolutely new-laid, twenty-four hours old being the best age, while they must have perfect shells. Badly-shelled ones should be used fresh. The best way of ensuring that only first-class eggs are preserved is to collect frequently (the weather may be freezing or there may be an incipient broody hen sitting in one of the nest-boxes which might ruin them), and then to sort them out. Dirty eggs do not preserve satisfactorily; they can be washed, but this destroys their keeping qualities. Finally, hold each egg up to a strong light between the thumbs and fingers of the two hands ; any minute cracks in the shell (it is surprising how many eggs are " starred " in cold weather) can then be seen. Such eggs should be used fresh.

Make up the preserving solution and pour some into the selected receptacle, but only a little if a wire basket is not fitted. Each day put in the surplus eggs from the gathering the day before and see that they are covered by at least 3 in. of the fluid. Fill the vessel only to within 3½ in. of the top, have 3 in. of fluid above the top layer and cover with a well-fitting lid or tie a piece of clean cloth round the top. Finally, keep the vessels in a room or shed with a fairly constant temperature of about 50 degrees F.

RABBITS FOR FLESH AND FUR

KEEPING rabbits is a sound proposition at any time, but particularly nowadays when the supply of meat is limited and prices are high. The majority of people appreciate a young rabbit when in good condition, and while one tends to grow tired of a constant repetition of the same dish, an occasional one is nearly always welcome.

Rabbits can be fed at practically no cost on the war-time allotment or garden plot, since for the most part they thrive on green food in variety. There should be ample supplies of such food all the year round if a satisfactory cropping plan is followed in the vegetable garden.

HOUSING FOR RABBITS

WHEN rabbits are kept on a large scale it is usual to erect a shed and place the hutches inside. This is not advised when only a few animals are kept, because the number of youngsters produced would not warrant going to such a cost. Outdoor hutches, so long as they are really well made, are as satisfactory as indoor ones, while the rabbits thrive quite as well, provided the hutches face towards the west and are not in the direct sunshine as they would be if facing south.

If the suggested layout shown in Fig. 1 has been adopted for the garden or allotment, the two lots of three-tier outside hutches can be put on the west side of the poultry house and the west side of the general-purpose shed. These are most convenient positions, as the sheds are of the correct depth to accommodate the type of hutch recommended.

TO CONSTRUCT A SET OF THREE HUTCHES

Fig. 9 gives an excellent idea of how a set of three hutches should be constructed. It may be thought that they are somewhat elaborate, but this is certainly not the case, seeing that breeding does will be kept in some of them—all of them at different times—and rabbits, as all other animals and birds, cannot give a good account of themselves when overcrowded.

Really good timber should be used ; the best is 1-in. tongued and grooved boarding. Remember when buying this that narrow boards are always cheaper than wide ones, so take those from 4 in. to 5 in. in width rather than those 10 in. or more. The framework is best constructed of 1½ in. by 1½ in. battens for the four corner uprights, and the bottom and top horizontals, but 1½ in. by 1 in. material may be used for the rest of the frame.

The bottom of the lowest hutch should be 9 in. from the ground. This involves a little stooping, but that cannot be avoided. The series of hutches should be 5½ ft. long, and each one 2 ft. high and 2 ft. from front to back. They should be divided into two compartments, plus a green-food and hay-rack. The smaller compartment, on the left of the illustration, should be 15 in. long, the larger section 3 ft. 9 in. long and the hay-rack 6 in.

The smaller compartment, which is really the sleeping-place, should have a solid door and the partition between the two sections should also be solid, save for the opening shown, which should be placed at the front.

If possible, the partition between the run and the hay-rack should be made of ¼-in. iron bars, placed 2 in. apart, but very stout wire may be used, as it costs less money. The front of the hay-rack should be solid but, like the front of the sleeping section, it should, of course, be hinged.

The front of the run compartment should be made as shown, the whole being hinged, but there should be an extra door, placed towards the top, for use when the doe is occupying the hutch together with her litter—it prevents the youngsters falling out as they might if the whole door is opened.

KEEPING THE HUTCH CLEAN AND SWEET

The most satisfactory litter is sawdust, but as rabbits void a considerable quantity of urine the floor should be thoroughly well tarred or painted, in order to prevent the liquid soaking in and making the hutch evil-smelling. The correct depth for the litter is 1 in. in the sleeping section, while a little heap should be made in the corner frequented by the rabbit. Saw-dust could be obtained at a nominal price in pre-war days ; it is still obtainable, though a little more is usually asked for it. If there are no local saw-mills or carpenters' shops in the neighbourhood, dry earth can be used as litter, but this is not so good. In any case, a very light sprinkling of disin-fectant powder should be mixed with the litter, whether it consists of sawdust or dry earth.

No provision need be made for a nest for the doe ; before kindling she will take hay from the rack and make her own.

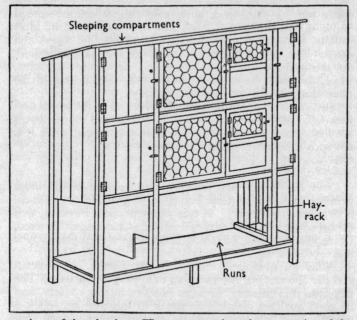

Sleeping compartments

Hay-rack

Runs

9. *A set of three hutches. The upper two show the construction of the doors, with special small doors for opening when the hutch contains a litter. The bottom hutch is shown without doors, revealing the interior of the sleeping compartment, run, and hay rack.*

BREEDS TO CHOOSE

THE different breeds of rabbit can be divided into three classes. There are those which are only useful for the production of flesh, the pelts selling for no more than those of wild rabbits. In the second class there are those which are bred principally for their pelts, some of these realising quite a high price at certain seasons of the year. Lastly, we have dual-purpose breeds—excellent for eating and with pelts which command a fair price when dried and sold in a good market.

The secret of successful rabbit-keeping is maintaining a pure breed. With some animals, such as goats, a cross is recommended, but not so with rabbits whose good characteristics are weakened, rather than strengthened, by crossing.

BREEDS FOR THE TABLE

Flesh breeds include the English, Flemish Giant, Belgian Hare and Japanese. The last-mentioned, by the way, find a ready sale as pets, since their colouring is unique—broad bands of black and red. But they are also excellent table rabbits, so any not sold as pets can always be killed and eaten. The three first-named breeds are very prolific indeed, for the average litter numbers round about eight or nine, while, as would be expected seeing that they belong to the table class, they fatten well and quickly.

Just one word regarding the English. It is the smallest of them all, but this is compensated for by the fact that its bones are lighter and there is less offal when paunching, while it is not such a hearty eater as the other two.

BREEDS FOR FUR

The fur breeds are certainly not recommended under present conditions because luxury buying, while not banned, is reduced considerably. It may be mentioned, however, that the breeds in this class are the Argente de Champagne, Beveren, Chinchilla, Havana, Lilac and Sitka, with the Angora, which is a wool-bearing rabbit.

Although numbered among the fur breeds, the Beveren and the Havana are two excellent dual-purpose varieties. The first-named is possibly the most popular in this country, and its good qualities certainly entitle it to this position. It is a grand rabbit, not only from the furriers' point of view, but because its table qualities approach those of the English. There are two colours—the blue and the white—and they are striking in appearance, particularly the blue. The colour is an intense shade of lavender blue throughout. The white is equally good, although not quite so attractive.

The Havana is a deep rich brown colour as a rule, but it varies from ruddy chocolate to dark coffee with an under-colour of pearl-grey. The pelts are always in demand, since they do not require dyeing, while the carcasses are first-class.

The war-time rabbit-keeper cannot do better than choose the Beveren because it cannot be beaten for its grand all-round qualities, while being a popular breed it is not difficult to obtain the necessary animals with which to make a start.

TO BREED AND REAR RABBITS

THE best time for making a start is in the spring, for this is, of course, the natural breeding season. There is, however, no great difficulty in breeding the whole year round, a necessity since a succession of carcasses is wanted for home consumption —provided the owner possesses the knowledge and is willing to give the animals the attention they require.

Since the object is to produce first-class table rabbits, the breeding age should be considered. A doe may be mated when she is about 16 to 18 weeks old, but it is infinitely better to postpone mating until she is some seven months. The progeny from young does are not quite so easy to rear, while the active breeding life of the doe is reduced. If she is mated at seven months the doe is useful as a breeder until she is between two and a half and three years old.

The breeders must be in first-class condition—not over-fat, but hard and firm, healthy and active, and this applies to the buck as much as to the does.

WHEN THE DOE SHOULD BE MATED

As with all animals, the doe can only be mated when she is in season. It is not difficult to determine when she is ready for mating, because she is restless, she stamps her hind feet on the floor, she takes hay from the rack and she often plucks fur off her chest. This is the time she should be put into the buck's cage—one of the hutches should be allocated to the male—and, an important point, the buck should not be put into the doe's hutch. At this time the animals should be watched ; when contact is over the male falls over on his side. The doe should then be transferred to her own hutch immediately.

Thirty to thirty-one days is the gestation period. In the case of very young or very old does it may be slightly longer, but neither of these should be used.

CARE OF THE DOE IN KINDLE

When kindling is approaching the doe starts to pluck the fur from her chest, flanks and belly. At this time a goodly quantity of hay should be put into the rack so that plenty of nesting material is available. Clean the hutch thoroughly at the same time, because no chance will offer itself for some time afterwards. When cleaning the hutch remove the doe to a vacant one—always carry rabbits by holding the ears in one hand and supporting the haunches with the other—and when everything is ready return her to the home to which she has grown accustomed.

It is advisable to keep a strict record of mating dates, because when the doe is due to kindle she must be left severely alone. If you open the door of the hutch to see how she is getting on she may kill all her young. Some few days after-wards, however, it is quite in order to look to see how things are progressing. Rabbits dislike the human smell, so before examining the contents of the sleeping compartment rub the hands with a little of the sawdust from the floor of the hutch.

A good doe can usually manage to feed eight or nine youngsters if she is in good condition ; should there be more it is advisable to remove the extra ones and kill them, since otherwise the whole of the litter would suffer from lack of food.

FEEDING AND WEANING THE LITTER

The doe should be allowed to look after her litter in her own way. Should she prove to be a bad mother she should not be mated again. Nothing is really required of the attendant until weaning time comes round.

When the youngsters are two or three weeks old they usually start nibbling at the food provided for their mother, but it is a mistake to imagine from this that they are capable of fending for themselves ; they cannot do so until they are about seven weeks old in winter and about six weeks old in summer. The young rabbits not only require their mother's milk, but they also stand in need of the heat of her body at night, particularly when outdoor hutches are used. The greater the amount of artificial food the young rabbits eat before weaning the better, because the change over to supplied food is less drastic.

When weaning time is due the doe should be removed to another hutch and the youngsters allowed to continue in occupation of the hutch to which they are used. For some weeks it is better to keep the whole litter together for separating them may cause them to go off their food, so the rapid growth which is desired does not materialise. When fourteen to fifteen weeks old the sexes may be separated if any of the males are required for stock purposes ; otherwise this is not necessary.

TO FEED RABBITS IN WAR-TIME

WHATEVER kind of stock is kept, the question of feeding is always a rather difficult one in war-time when supplies of the more common foods are reduced. In the case of rabbits, the difficulty is not a serious one, because practically no kind of food comes amiss. All kinds of garden produce can be used with good results ; this includes greens, pea-pods, pea and bean haulm, carrot tops, turnip tops, lettuces, beet leaves, and even lawn mowings if you are sufficiently fortunate to have any available. Roots are particularly useful whether carrots, potatoes, parsnips, beets or any other. It is usually possible, too, to find a lot of food in the hedgerows, such as coltsfoot, dandelion, groundsel, march mallow, shepherd's purse and plantain. Care must be taken, however, not to pick green stuff too near the roadside, where it may have been fouled by dogs or other animals, since this might prove disastrous to your stock.

At the same time, a certain amount of dry food is necessary. The staple grain is oats, while bran, hay, acorns, malt culms, brewers' grains, oatmeal, linseed and barley meal, together with straw, are also excellent. A bigger proportion of dry food is required in the winter than in the summer.

The same rule applies to feeding rabbits as to other forms of live stock—regular feeding hours must be kept. Rabbits may be fed twice or three times a day ; at 8 a.m. and 6 p.m., if twice, or 8 a.m., noon and 6 p.m., if three times. Proper earthenware troughs should be used, but long metal-flanged wooden ones are nearly as good. Provide plenty of fresh drinking water every day.

As previously mentioned, many different foods can be fed to rabbits, but it may be helpful if a few rations are suggested, since these will serve as a guide.

During the period before the doe kindles she may be given green food and hay first thing in the morning ; more green food at noon ; and either a good mash or a handful of oats with a further supply of hay and green food in the late afternoon or evening.

Good feeding is essential after kindling, and the doe should be allowed the chance of getting a few wisps of hay whenever she feels inclined ; the rack should be kept supplied, but only small quantities should be put in at a time, so that it is always fresh and sweet. For a morning meal there is nothing better than green food, with the same kind of food in the evening. At noon, however, something more substantial is required, so a good mash should be provided.

Two days a week crushed oats may be given in place of the mash, which can well consist of equal parts of ground oats, middlings, bran and barley meal—foods at present available and likely to be so in future.

EXTRA FOOD FOR YOUNG RABBITS

The growing rabbits, after weaning, should be fed liberally on green food and hay or dried grass in the morning, a little stale bread if available and more green food at midday, and crushed oats or mash, together with hay and green food, in the evening. When feeding the young rabbits for the last two weeks before killing, the morning feed may consist of cooked potatoes, dried off with middlings or barley meal, green food and hay ; a few oats, green food and hay should be provided at noon ; and a good mash of barley meal and middlings with still more hay and green food should be given at night.

KILLING AND SKINNING

BEFORE killing, rabbits should be starved for twenty-four hours. Killing is best carried out by holding the animal up by the back legs and giving it a sharp knock on the back of the neck, just behind the ears ; a hard knock is necessary to kill, for a light one only stuns the animal.

When killed a slit should be made in the left leg, between the bone and the tendon, and the right foot passed through so that it can be hung up easily.

Paunching is the next task. Make a slit some 4 in. in length along the centre of the belly towards the hindquarters, then the stomach, etc., can be removed. The heart, liver and lungs are not taken out by this operation ; they can be left in their natural position.

TO REMOVE AND DRY THE PELT

Skinning comes next. Press the skin from the flank and work the fingers and thumb towards the hindquarters, at the same time pulling the skin. Push the leg through the skin and give the skin a sharp pull so that it breaks away at the hock. Deal with the other hind leg in the same manner. Pull the skin with both hands towards the front until it is removed as far as the ears. Cut off the ears close to the head, cut over the eyes and with the knife remove the skin from the head.

If the pelts are to be sold they should be dried, but not cured. To dry, use drawing-pins to fasten the pelts firmly to a flat board, with the fur side downwards. If possible, dry in the open air, but the shed does well enough in bad weather. After a day and a night scrape the skin and take away all fat adhering, a blunt knife being the best instrument to use. Then continue drying until completed.

If skins have to be kept for some time, until a sufficient number has been obtained to warrant sending them to the furriers, they are best stored back to back in a dry, well-ventilated shed ; a sprinkle of naphthalene proves beneficial.

TREATING SICK RABBITS

COLDS.—These are due to damp, draughty hutches, together with bad ventilation. The symptoms are running at the eyes and nose, inflammation of the eyes and sneezing. Keep the animal warm, give one or two feeds of warm milk, and bathe the eyes once a day with a lotion consisting of 2 grains of sulphate of zinc in 1 oz. of water.

COUGHS.—Due to the same causes as colds and to neglected colds. The symptoms are moping, coughing and possibly the usual symptoms of a cold. Treat as for colds, but in severe cases add 6 drops of sweet spirits of nitre to the milk.

COLIC.—This is usually the result of feeding unsuitable food. Uneasiness, pain and a swollen body are symptoms. Give a teaspoonful of castor oil and massage the stomach gently until the pain is relieved.

CONSTIPATION.—Lack of green food and keeping in a too-small hutch with consequent lack of exercise cause constipation. Mix a small quantity of flowers of sulphur in the mash, and give a teaspoonful of castor oil if the case is a severe one.

DIARRHŒA.—A probable cause is the feeding of stale green food. The droppings are loose and watery and the animal quickly loses flesh. Feed on dry food for a time, and in bad cases give five or six grains of precipitated chalk, and return to normal feeding gradually.

INSECT PESTS.—Dirty, damp hutches with dirty litter are the usual cause. Dullness and thinness are symptoms, while insects are found round the ears and forehead. Rub with flowers of sulphur and dust it into corners of the hutch.

LIVER DISEASE.—This may be the result of using related does and buck, of unwholesome food, of bad sanitary conditions or of improper housing. The eyes are usually bright and glassy, appetite is abnormally large, condition poor, backbone prominent yet the stomach is distended. Kill and bury.

MANGE.—This is a contagious disease due to lack of green food and dirty hutches. The hair falls out freely and the skin becomes scaly. Rub the affected parts every third day with a mixture of lard, 2 parts ; sulphur, 1 part.

REDWATER.—This is caused by dampness, exposure and improper feeding. The urine appears to be tinged with blood and there is general mopishness. Give barley water to drink with 4 drops of sweet spirits of nitre every morning until cured.

SLOBBERS.—Again damp and draughty hutches are the principal cause. The only symptom is a running at the mouth. Wash the mouth out three times a day with a solution of alum and every third day sprinkle flowers of sulphur in the mash.

BEES TO GIVE HONEY AND FINE FRUIT

Every allotment-holder and home gardener should invest in one or more hives of bees, not only for the honey they produce, but because bees are indispensable for fertilising many kinds of flowers, especially fruit blossom. Thus, the products of the hives will not only help to eke out your sugar ration in wartime but the bees will help to provide you with better blooms and heavier crops of fruit.

The proximity of flowers and other plants is essential for honey-production, so bee-keeping cannot be carried on in an uncultivated town garden. Nectar gathered from fruit blossom produces a light-coloured, early harvest of honey, while that obtained from heather is dark-coloured and late-maturing. Nectar is also obtained, of course, from cultivated flowers, but wild field plants, such as white clover, mustard and rape will yield plentiful supplies, as well as lime trees. In the spring, when other flowers are not available, wallflowers, crocuses, mignonette and so on should be grown near the hive to provide the necessary pollen—a staple part of the bees' food. When natural sources of pollen fail, the nitrogen content must be supplied in artificial form, such as pea flour, sprinkled on dry straw in boxes.

TREATMENT FOR STINGS

If the bees are handled as suggested, the keeper will rarely, if ever, be stung. To treat a sting, should it occur, the sting itself should first be removed by squeezing it out and ammonia applied, unless the injured part is near the eye, ear, nose or mouth. In this case, apply a solution of common salt, permanganate of potash or bicarbonate of soda. A number of really bad stings require medical attention.

EQUIPMENT REQUIRED FOR BEE-KEEPING

No expensive outlay is necessary to start bee-keeping. A single hive, complete with colony, purchased in the spring, can be used to build up fresh stocks as required. All that is needed is : the hive ; feeding vessels ; feeding bottle ; one or two skeps ; smoker ; frames and sections for the bees to fill with honey, if the hive is not already equipped with these when bought ; protective veil and gloves.

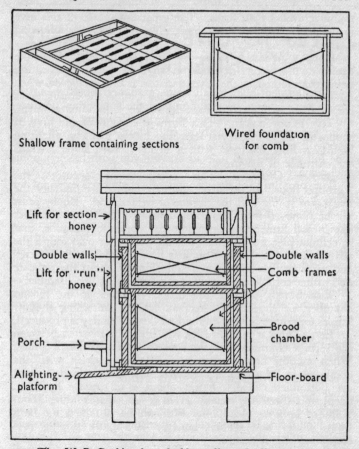

Shallow frame containing sections

Wired foundation for comb

Lift for section honey

Double walls

Lift for "run" honey

Double walls

Comb frames

Brood chamber

Porch

Alighting-platform

Floor-board

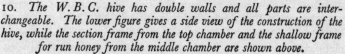

10. *The W. B. C. hive has double walls and all parts are inter-changeable. The lower figure gives a side view of the construction of the hive, while the section frame from the top chamber and the shallow frame for run honey from the middle chamber are shown above.*

HOW THE HIVE IS CONSTRUCTED

It is possible for any one who is handy with tools to make a hive, but the beekeeper who is just beginning is advised to buy his first one from a reliable dealer in bee appliances. If, when he wants another, he feels inclined to make it himself, he can then model it on the one he has bought and found to be satisfactory.

The best type of hive is that known as the W.B.C., a type

manufactured by all firms. The great advantage of this hive is that all parts are interchangeable. It has the following features :

DOUBLE WALLS.—These are most important, since the health of the colony depends on an even warm temperature being maintained in the hive, and this is only achieved when the walls do not conduct heat. In the winter, the double walls can be filled with chaff or cork dust to keep the inmates warm.

THE FLOOR-BOARD.—This forms the stand of the hive, is supported on four splayed legs, and has in front an alighting board—a little platform with a slight upward slope towards the entrance of the hive.

BROOD CHAMBER.—This compartment occupies the " ground floor " of the hive, and here combs are built for the rearing of young and the storage of winter food. Honey must not be removed from this compartment. The brood chamber has special fitments to accommodate comb foundations, that is, cellular pieces of beeswax, but the beekeeper who adopts the advice given here to buy his first hive complete with fitments and working bees need not trouble himself about the delicate and rather complicated operation of furnishing this chamber.

THE SUPER.—Above the brood chamber is the second chamber, or super as beekeepers call it, containing shallow frames for combs in which liquid, or " run," honey is produced.

LIFT.—This is really a rack which can be inserted between the second chamber and the roof to hold additional combs. When section honey—that is, thick honey eaten with the comb—is to be produced, sections must be provided. These are bottomless wooden boxes, about 4 in. square by 2 in. deep, and there are usually 21 in a lift, each holding about 1 lb. of honey. Additional lifts can be obtained for both frame honey and section honey. A slightly sloping roof completes the structure.

OUTFIT FOR FEEDING AND HANDLING

FEEDING VESSELS.—It is not necessary to buy a number of elaborate utensils for holding water and any artificial dry foods that may be necessary, though there are many on the market. A few shallow pans will be quite suitable as water containers. They should be kept very clean, the water changed two or three times a day, and little pebbles or sticks placed in them to enable the bees to alight and drink without risk of drowning. Keep them on a stand near the hive.

FEEDING BOTTLE.—This appliance is for feeding the bees with prepared syrup when their own stores of food are insufficient. A graduated bottle feeder, with slots through which the syrup slowly runs, can be purchased, but a feeder may be improvised by filling a glass jam jar with the feeding syrup, covering the top with two thicknesses of muslin, and inverting it on a piece of fine zinc placed over the feeding hole, which is the bees' access to their stores of honey.

SKEPS.—Straw or wicker beehives, which have now been superseded by the modern wooden hives described, were known as skeps. A new swarm may arrive in a skep, and will require to be transferred to a hive. The term also applies to wooden or wicker baskets, in which the bees can be collected at swarming times, and two or three of these should always be on hand.

VEIL AND GLOVES.—As the beekeeper becomes more experienced in handling his charges and discards all fear of stings (it is amazing how bees seem to sense timidity in those who approach them, and to take advantage of it), he can and certainly should discard the gloves, since wearing them must result in a certain amount of clumsiness and this annoys the insects. Until then, wear gloves as thin as possible, consistent with protection. A veil for protecting the face and neck is essential, particularly for a woman, for bees are apt to settle in the hair, and may sting in their efforts to free themselves. A piece of black mosquito-netting, threaded top and bottom with thin elastic, affords the best protection. It should completely cover face and neck, the top elastic fitting tightly round the crown of the head, and the bottom inside the collar. A hat should be worn over it.

SMOKER.—When you wish to examine the contents of the hive, the best way to control the bees is to blow a puff of smoke from a smoker sold for the purpose in their direction. This scares them, and when they are nervous they at once gorge themselves with food until they are in an amenable condition. They are best-tempered in warm, sunny weather.

TO CHOOSE YOUR STOCK

As with other kinds of stock, the strain (or pedigree) of bees is more important than the breed. What the apiarist expects of a swarm of honey bees is that they shall be prolific, hardy, first-class nectar gatherers and as nearly immune from disease as possible. There are a number of different races, including the English, Dutch, Italian, Cyprian, Holy Lands, Tunisian, Caucasian and Banat. The Dutch are specially popular on account of their comparative immunity to Isle of Wight disease, but a reliable strain of the English should possess all the desirable characteristics already mentioned.

WHEN CROSS-BREEDS ARE BETTER

Sometimes, however, it is difficult to obtain a really good strain of the common English, and in this case the advice of the vendor or of an experienced beekeeper in your district should be sought. There are excellent crosses between the English and one of the imported breeds to be obtained. In all probability your dealer will offer a cross between the English and Italian ; the latter imparts vigour and prolificness to the strain.

WHY A GOOD QUEEN BEE IS ESSENTIAL

A colony of bees normally numbers about 20,000 and consists of the queen, a large number of workers, which are undeveloped females, and a few male bees or drones. The queen bee is the mother of all the inmates of the hive, and so is responsible for the qualities in the progeny on which the beekeeper's success will depend. The size of the population of the hive depends on her prolificness, and its industry and disposition upon her own qualities in this direction. She differs from all other members of the colony in having shorter wings, and her body is narrower than that of the drone and shorter than the working bee's.

The queen is at her best during the second year, and should be discarded and a new queen procured in the third. The colony will itself breed a new queen, but if the inexperienced beekeeper has to make a choice of queens he should seek the advice of an expert apiarist.

If you wish to produce section honey, this fact should be mentioned when buying the bees, for some strains are not so suitable for this work as others. Perfect cleanliness and white capping—that is, the sealing of the cells when they are filled with honey—is essential for this work.

THREE WAYS OF BUYING STOCK

You should obtain your stock as early in the spring as possible and may do this in one of three ways : by buying a nucleus, that is, a few frames containing brood and food ; by buying a swarm of bees—i.e. bees which have just left the old hive to their growing progeny, and set out in search of a new home ; and a colony, which will already have started working and storing food. The cost of the latter will naturally be more than in the other two cases, but it is the method advised for the beginner, since otherwise he will have all the trouble of rearing the bees and introducing them to the hive.

FOOD FOR THE HONEY-MAKERS

ASSUMING, then, that a colony complete in hive has been bought about May, the beekeeper must see that the work of the hive is being properly carried out. The bees' duties consist of collecting pollen, water and nectar for food; of collecting nectar for honey and building storage combs to hold it ; of cleaning the cells for the queens to lay in, nursing and rearing the larvæ. The brood nest must be kept warm to encourage fertilization and rearing of young bees.

Feeding is one of the most important duties of the bee-keeper, since only by the provision of the right kind of food at the right times of the year can the colony be kept up to strength and in perfect condition.

A HOME-MADE SPRING STIMULANT

There is a period in the spring and early summer of every year called the honey-flow when the nectar is most abundant, and the beekeeper should know when this occurs in his district. Six weeks beforehand the bees should be stimulated by being given a special syrup for spring feeding. Such a stimulant is particularly necessary in those localities where the honey-flow is early. If there is any winter food left, a few inches of the white capping over the cells should be bruised daily until the bees have consumed it all. Fortunately, the Government, realising the importance of honey-production, allow beekeepers to purchase the sugar necessary for feeding purposes, so the syrup can be made without difficulty.

An excellent spring feeding syrup consists of 5 lb. of the best cane sugar (brown sugar should never be used), $3\frac{1}{2}$ pints water, a dessertspoon of vinegar, and a quarter of a teaspoon salt boiled together for a few minutes. It is advisable to medicate the syrup with some substance like naphthol beta or phenyl to guard against foul brood or with bacterol or dioxogen if it is known that Isle of Wight disease is or has been prevalent in the district. Allow 1 teaspoon to each pound of sugar. This mixture is given to the bees in the feeding bottle described in the list of equipment required, and all they need in addition is plenty of water in shallow vessels containing stones or sticks as alighting places. When the feeding bottle is emptied, it must be replenished.

TO MAKE AUTUMN SYRUP

The best syrup for autumn feeding is made as follows : Take 5 lb. of the best cane sugar, $2\frac{1}{2}$ pints of water, a dessert-spoon of vinegar, a small pinch of salt, and boil the whole lot together for a couple of minutes. Medicate the syrup in the same way as the spring feeding preparation.

When autumn feeding is carried out as suggested, the bees should come through the winter in fine fettle, and in the spring all they will want is the stimulant already suggested.

HARVESTING THE HONEY

THE frames and sections should be taken out of the hive as soon as they are properly sealed over. It is for the beekeeper to decide whether it will serve his requirements better to produce section or run honey or some of both. The majority of people prefer section honey, in which case the comb is eaten as well as the honey, but the one difficulty is that unless it is consumed fairly quickly there is always a danger that it granulates. Granulation can be prevented to some extent by storing the sections in a dry, fairly warm room or cupboard, but only for a limited length of time.

Frame honey is extracted, or " run," and a proper extractor is required. These machines are fairly expensive, but there is no need to buy one, because in most districts it is possible to hire one for the few days necessary for extraction. Enquiries should be made from the dealer in bee appliances, since he usually has one or two to loan.

When honey is extracted it is absolutely essential for the work to be done in a place which is proof against the entry not only of bees but all other insects. Bees appear to be able to trace the scent of honey to its source ; unless the place is proofed it will be invaded. The bees will take control, and when it is possible for the beekeeper to return to the scene of operations no honey will remain for human consumption.

When preparing run honey for sale, it is usual to sort over the combs according to colour, and as colour is always an important consideration, the same plan should be followed even when the honey is eaten at home. Light-coloured honey is usually better flavoured than the darker kinds, although the latter are excellent for sweetening various kinds of dishes for which sugar is normally used.

HOW TO EXTRACT RUN HONEY

The first job when extracting honey is to uncap the combs. This should be done with a special knife obtained when the extractor is hired. During the uncapping process the knife should be kept heated in very hot water, but dried before use. Cutting consists of a gentle sweep in an upward direction, the frame being held so that the sheet of capping falls at an angle from the comb; that is, it should be tilted inwards. Both sides must be uncapped at the same time, and when once completed the frame should be placed at once into the extractor. When the extractor cages are filled the handle should be turned at an even speed—the correct speed can be told by the sound of the honey being thrown against the wall of the machine. When one side has been fully extracted the frames should be turned round and the process repeated.

A honey-ripener can also be hired. A honey-ripener is a vessel with a strainer at the top and a tap at the bottom into which the honey in the extractor is drawn off when it reaches the level of the bottom of the cages. Both capping and run honey should be placed into the strainer and, when all the combs have been dealt with, should be allowed to remain in the ripener for about a week, so that any thin, unripe honey will rise to the top. When the best honey is run out of the machine the inferior and unusable stuff remains behind.

After extracting, the combs should be returned to the hive ; the bees appreciate the task of cleaning them up. Afterwards they can be stored for use the following year.

USES FOR BY-PRODUCTS OF THE HIVE

There is quite a good market for beeswax, as well as many uses for it in the home, so the cappings and various odd pieces of comb, including " brace-comb " and the short spurs often built in different parts of the hive, should be treated so that the wax is recovered. The pieces can be washed in rain water and then placed into the oven. A little water should be placed into the bottom of a basin and a sieve put over the top and the combs placed into this, but if there is no sieve, cheese-cloth may be used. The wax runs into the basin and all refuse material remains on top of the strainer. The wax can then be made up into small cakes or into one large one.

WHEN THE BEES SWARM

THE swarming of a colony—that is their emergence from the hive under the leadership of the queen to make a new home —takes place usually about May. This is called a first swarm, and after-swarms are called casts. If you are buying a swarm of bees and not a colony, always buy the first swarm, which should weigh about 5 lb. After-swarms weigh only about 2 lb. and have a virgin queen.

A new hive must be in readiness for the swarm, and the " emigrating " bees coaxed into it. When they leave the hive they will settle on a tree or branch, and should be shaken off into a clean skep. Turn the skep on its side on the ground, over which you have spread a clean cloth, and any flying bees will rejoin the swarm before nightfall.

When all have arrived, remove the skep, pick up the cloth gently, and then quickly tip the bees out on to a table placed in front of the hive and on a level with it. Guide a few bees through the entrance with a spoon and the others will quickly follow. See that the queen bee enters with the others. Ingress is made easier if the hive is tilted slightly upwards in front.

The emigrants will soon start work on the new combs, but they will need feeding with syrup during the first few days.

AILMENTS OF BEES

THE two principal troubles likely to be encountered by the beekeeper are foul brood and Isle of Wight disease. The former can be cured ; the latter cannot. Second-hand hives should not be bought, as they may carry infection. Napthalene sprinkled in the hive at intervals helps to prevent foul brood.

FOUL BROOD.—If your stocks show lack of energy, and seem to have little desire to fly or swarm, inspect the combs at once. If foul brood is present you will find dead and dying larvæ, and others with their covers sunken or perforated. The larvæ turn either pale yellow and then brown, or first grey and then nearly black. Destroy bees, combs, frames and quilts. The hive must be thoroughly disinfected before using again.

It may be possible to save some of the inmates of an infected colony if it is strong, by making them swarm artificially into a skep or box. Keep them confined in a cool place for two complete days. During this time they will consume all the honey they have taken with them, and the diseased bees will have died. Paint the outside of the hive with oil paint.

When the bees have been confined for two days, remove them to a movable comb hive, and feed them for at least a week on syrup containing napthol beta. In the case of mild attacks, disinfection with formaldehyde may be sufficient. Try to obtain the assistance of an expert apiarist when you have to carry out this treatment for the first time.

ISLE OF WIGHT DISEASE.—Bees afflicted with this disease may be seen on fine days crawling on the ground unable to fly. Also, the combs and entrances may be soiled. As already stated, this is incurable, but it may be prevented by feeding the stocks in winter on a preparation of bacteriolized candy.

Prescriptions and information on technical points can be ﻪtained from leaflets issued by the Ministry of Agriculture.